POLICE ETHICS

ABOUT THE AUTHOR

Dr. Tom Barker is a Professor of Criminal Justice at Eastern Kentucky University. He is the former Dean of the College of Criminal Justice at Jacksonville State University in Jacksonville, Alabama. A former police officer and a certified police academy instructor, Dr. Barker has been conducting research on police corruption and police misconduct for over thirty years. He has written six books and over twenty articles on these topics. In addition, he has conducted numerous workshops and seminars for a variety of police agencies throughout the United States on ethical issues in law enforcement. Dr. Barker has served as an expert witness in both federal and state courts on police ethical behavior on numerous occasions.

Dr. Barker is a past president of the Academy of Criminal Justice Sciences (1987–1988) and the Southern Criminal Justice Association (1984–1985). He has received numerous awards, including the Founders Award from both the Academy of Criminal Justice Sciences and the Southern Criminal Justice Association.

Third Edition

POLICE ETHICS

Crisis in Law Enforcement

By

TOM BARKER, PH.D.

*Professor of Criminal Justice
College of Justice and Safety
Department of Criminal Justice
Eastern Kentucky University
Richmond, Kentucky*

CHARLES C THOMAS • PUBLISHER, LTD.
Springfield • Illinois • U.S.A.

Published and Distributed Throughout the World by

CHARLES C THOMAS • PUBLISHER, LTD.
2600 South First Street
Springfield, Illinois 62704

This book is protected by copyright. No part of
it may be reproduced in any manner without written
permission from the publisher. All rights reserved.

© 2011 by CHARLES C THOMAS • PUBLISHER, LTD.

ISBN 978-0-398-08615-2 (hard)
ISBN 978-0-398-08616-9 (paper)
ISBN 978-0-398-08617-6 (e-book)

Library of Congress Catalog Card Number: 2010033630

With THOMAS BOOKS *careful attention is given to all details of manufacturing and design. It is the Publisher's desire to present books that are satisfactory as to their physical qualities and artistic possibilities and appropriate for their particular use.* THOMAS BOOKS *will be true to those laws of quality that assure a good name and good will.*

*Printed in the United States of America
SM-R-3*

Library of Congress Cataloging-in-Publication Data

Barker, Tom, Ph.D.
  Police ethics : crisis in law enforcement / by Tom Barker. -- 3rd ed.
    p. cm.
  Includes bibliographical references and index.
  ISBN 978-0-398-08615-2 (hard) -- ISBN 978-0-398-08616-9 (pbk.)
  1. Police ethics--United States. 2. Law enforcement--United States. I. Title.
  HV7924.B37 2011
  174'.93632--dc22

2010033630

PREFACE

The objective of this third edition is the same as it was for the first edition and the second: to provide law enforcement officers and law enforcement supervisors with an understanding of ethical behavior as it relates to the police occupation. The book is based on the premise that an ethical crisis has always existed in law enforcement and is the result of the nature of the police occupation; policing is and always has been a *morally dangerous occupation.*

The nature of police duties combined with the inherent power of the position insures that policing will always be morally dangerous for those who choose to join the occupation no matter how noble their intentions. Recognizing this fact is the key to understanding police ethical behavior.

Once we understand the moral dangers of the occupation, we can appreciate how important ethical standards are for police officers. If law enforcement is ever going to be recognized as a profession, we have to ensure that the behavior of all law enforcement officers (municipal, county, state, federal, and special district) conform to recognized ethical standards. The author hopes that this book will serve as a guide for new officers and a refresher for experienced officers as we move the occupation forward and make policing a profession that is real and not rhetoric.

T.B.

CONTENTS

	Page
Preface	v

Chapter

1. POLICING – A MORALLY DANGEROUS OCCUPATION ... 3
2. PROFESSIONAL/OCCUPATIONAL ETHICS ... 15
3. LAW ENFORCEMENT CODE OF ETHICS – PARAGRAPH 1 ... 20
4. LAW ENFORCEMENT CODE OF ETHICS – PARAGRAPH 2 ... 25
5. LAW ENFORCEMENT CODE OF ETHICS – PARAGRAPH 3 ... 31
6. LAW ENFORCEMENT CODE OF ETHICS – PARAGRAPH 4 AND 5 ... 35
7. MAJOR LAW ENFORCEMENT ETHICAL VIOLATIONS ... 37
8. POLICE CORRUPTION ... 60
9. CORRUPT PRACTICES AND CORRUPTION CONTROL ... 74
10. ABUSE OF AUTHORITY ... 107
11. CONTROLLING POLICE UNETHICAL BEHAVIOR ... 126
12. CONCLUSION ... 143

References ... 147
Index ... 157

POLICE ETHICS

Chapter 1

POLICING – A MORALLY DANGEROUS OCCUPATION

INTRODUCTION

Since the publication of the first edition of this book in 1996, the reported instances of unethical behavior (criminal and noncriminal) by law enforcement officers at all levels of government have continued and become more visible. One of the traditional explanations for police unethical behavior has been that police-citizen confrontational encounters occur alone and unobserved – under a cloud of secrecy. For the most part, that is not true today. In the age of cell phones, surveillance cameras, dash cam recorders, and other video equipment, police abuse when it occurs has become more visible and disturbing. Videos showing instances of police use of excessive force are posted on the Internet and shown on the news before police supervisors are notified and can open an investigation. The cell-phone video of the shooting of an unarmed man on a train platform by a Bay Area Rapid Transit Police Officer in 2009 was widely circulated on the Internet and on news shows before the department started an investigation. Protests and riots quickly erupted in and around Oakland, California. The officer is currently on trial. YouTube has brought more attention to police unethical behavior than any government commission. The police officer of today must assume that any action he or she takes will be videotaped and posted on some website. It is amazing that police officers engage in egregious behavior when they know or should know that bystanders are taking pictures or videos. On March 3, 2010, after Maryland's basketball team defeated Duke, police were called out to control the jubilant crowd. Students can be seen holding up their cell-phones, taking pictures or videos of the police and the celebration. Several officers were caught on video beating a University of Maryland student with nightsticks (Hayes, 2010). The video clearly repudiates the officers' original account of the incident. The student beaten by the officers was arrested and charged with assaulting mounted officers. The tape contradicts this "cover-up" attempt and the charges were dropped. The police spokesman is quoted as saying "Not only is the conduct of the officers on tape excessive – and it's clearly excessive –" there are other issues to address. The chief was quoted as saying he was outraged. One officer has been suspended and the prosecutor is investigating the incident. The FBI is also investigating the incident for civil rights violations. The Civil Rights Division of the Department of Justice is becoming more aggressive in the investigation and prosecution of law enforcement officers at all levels of government, as can be gauged by the numerous Department of Justice Press Releases cited in this edition.

Videos and surveillance cameras have demonstrated that on occasion law enforcement officers have lied and falsely arrested subjects. Two Detroit officers received three years probation after a gas station's security video showed they falsely accused a man of the possession of marijuana and carrying a concealed weapon (Swickard, 2010). The family of the victim, believing his protestations of innocence, found the video. Prosecutors in Columbia, South Carolina dropped the charge of resisting arrest against an attorney because the three officers involved refused to testify, fearing their testimony would incriminate them (Smith, 2010). State police are investigating the incident and surveillance videotape does not support the officers' story.

The police misuse of "nonlethal" weapons such as the TASER and chemical sprays is open to public scrutiny. The TASER is marketed as a low-level use of force, but the public does not see it that way. Continued misuse – horseplay on each other and relatives; use/misuse on children, some younger than ten; use/misuse on dead, unconscious, deaf, non-English-speaking subjects; use/misuse on handcuffed prisoners as punishment or retaliation; overuse (on any level of noncompliance), etc. – of what can be useful nonlethal weapons will result in severe restrictions or prohibition. A Naples, Florida officer was caught on tape zapping a female colleague with a TASER. Three Gwinnett County Police officers resigned, two in lieu of termination and the third before his arrest, after a TASER incident involving a Waffle House Employee (Simmons, 2009). All three officers were regular customers where they received free food, in violation of department rules. One officer tasered the employee as a prank while the other two, both sergeants, watched. The officer that tasered the employee has been indicted for aggravated assault and violation of oath of office (Estep, 2010). In an effort to reduce public criticism, many departments are using the TASER as a defensive tool and not an offensive weapon and allowing it to be used only when the non-compliant subject poses a threat to the officers, citizens, or suspect.

Videos often do not tell the whole story surrounding questionable police actions. And, there is no doubt that any force, especially the use of weapons is never pretty whether it is necessary or unnecessary. The 2006 videotape of a Bernardino County Sheriff's Deputy shooting an unarmed Air Force military police officer was touted as an obvious instance of police brutality on the Internet and police misconduct websites, but a jury took barely two hours to acquit the former deputy of all charges (Brooks & Gang, 2007). In 2008, a group of Philadelphia police officers were caught on camera from a news helicopter kicking and punching three suspects after a long police chase. After the tape became national news, the chief fired four officers. Subsequently a grand jury cleared the officers of any crimes and an arbitrator ruled that the officer should get their jobs back (Masterson, 2010). The Philadelphia chief of police is often accused of having a "no nonsense" policy on police misconduct and firing officers when a lesser punishment is indicated.

There is no doubt that videotapes put the police on the defensive, create a skeptical public damaging police community relations, and increase the likelihood of successful civil actions. Police spokespersons do not help the occupation or their department by "stonewalling" or responding with "no comments" to valid inquiries into these incidents. There is nothing to gain from a police community relations standpoint to arrest those videotaping the police or asking for laws to make the taping illegal. After all, the police in a free society have been and always will be accountable for their actions.

There should be renewed efforts by law enforcement executives and professional associations to ensure that the **Law Enforcement Code of Ethics** is a valid standard for ethical police conduct. The Code must be more than rhetoric and if it is no longer valuable as standard of conduct, then it should be changed, updated, or become a part of police history. Police policy, formal or informal, should not condone behavior that violates the ethical standards such as gratuities or violations of constitutional rights.

Recent events suggest that the nature of corrupt practices has changed, particularly in some large urban police departments with histories of systematic corruption. In these departments, the corrupt acts appear to be the result of "rotten apples" and "rotten groups" engaging primarily in drug-related crimes (Barker, 2002). These crimes include officers operating as gangs of robbers in uniform or outfitting crews of robbers with police equipment – raid jackets, badges, handcuffs, and bullet-resistant vests (Sulzerberger, May 13, 2010). Some of these "badge packing" criminals are very dangerous men and women who will kill (and have killed) fellow cops and civilians. Examples of these criminal law enforcement officers are provided in this edition.

Corrupt practices occur in federal law enforcement agencies as drug trafficking has expanded. What is known as the *Crispin Case* is an example. Margarita Crispin, a corrupt Border Control Inspector, allowed illegal drug traffickers to move illegal drugs across the U.S.-Mexican Border through her border post in El Paso, Texas (DOJ, 06/08/09). This case points out that changing times create new opportunities for police misconduct. The increased efforts to secure our borders after 9/11 have not only created new opportunities for corruption, but they have introduced a new threat – terrorists or weapons of mass destruction being allowed into the country by a corrupt or cooperating border agent/s.

The specter of police departments with system-wide problems still exists, especially in those departments with long histories of police corruption, such as New Orleans. A 1993 undercover FBI investigation into police corruption in New Orleans, dubbed Operation Shattered Shield, led to the conviction of ten NOPD officers, including one who was sentenced to death for ordering a hit on a woman who filed a civil rights complaint against him. Reforms instituted after this operation evidently did not solve the problem. A recent New Orleans *Times-Picayune* editorial calls the NOPD "one of the least effective and *most corrupt police forces* in the nation" (*Times-Picayune*, 2010). Police misconduct incidents following Hurricane Katrina, especially the killing of two innocent civilians on the Danziger Bridge, and the subsequent cover-up, support this indictment of the NOPD. Four New Orleans police officers pleaded guilty to federal charges involving the cover-up of the Danziger shootings. A fifth officer recently pleaded guilty to writing a false charging document and lying to investigators and a grand jury. This officer admitted that the officers involved entered into a conspiracy to provide false and misleading information so that the shootings would appear justified and shield the officers involved from any liability (DOJ, June 4, 2010).

Three current and two former members of the New Orleans Police Department have been indicted by a federal grand jury following another post-Katrina incident (DOJ, 2010). The eleven-count indictment is in connection with the shooting and burning of the victim's body three days after Hurricane Katrina. The allegations are that the police officers, including three lieutenants, shot and killed the victim, burned his body and car, assaulted civilians who tried to help the victim, and engaged in a cover-up of the incident.

New Orleans' new mayor has asked for the U.S. Department of Justice to help the city address and prevent police misconduct (Schoichet, 2010). The Department of Justice has announced that it will open a "pattern or practice" investigation into misconduct in the NOPD that will result in a consent decree between the DOJ and the NOPD. Ongoing federal investigations into other shootings and corruption allegations will serve as the platform for reform by the new mayor and police chief.

The instances of Noble Cause Injustice (using unlawful means to control crime) are, unfortunately, all too common, particularly in the real or perceived war on drugs. Some officers who see themselves as "good" cops will conduct illegal searches and seizures, falsely swear to obtain warrants, plant evidence, and lie in court to put away the "dirt bags." The "Worst Case Scenario" of Noble Cause Injustice occurred in Atlanta, Georgia, where drug officers executing an illegal search warrant shot and killed a 92-year-old grandmother and then planted dope in the house and falsified reports to cover-up their misdeeds. Four police officers are in prison, two have been fired, six have been disciplined, and one has resigned as a result of the federal and state investigation that followed. As happened in Atlanta, fellow officers, knowing that these practices occur, remain silent out of a false sense of loyalty. However, as I have repeatedly said in training sessions, there is never an ethical officer observing the unethical, illegal, corrupt, or brutal behavior of a fellow officer without taking some action. The innocent are convicted and killed as police officers fight the war on crime with illegal or questionable means armed with a false sense that bad can come from evil.

Prior to the publication of the first edition, all of us in the police community were appalled by the actions of LAPD officers (the participants and observers) during the videotaped beating of Rodney King. Numerous videotapes of other officers engaging in questionable and obvious acts of brutality/misconduct have appeared since then. An intoxicated off-duty Chicago police officer beating a female bartender and the tape of a police officer slamming a teenager on the hood of a police car and punching him were shown over and over again. As I write this, a videotape of a Seattle officer stomping the head and body of a young man while using racial epithets is being shown on news broadcasts nationally and internationally. The officer can be clearly heard saying, "I'm going to beat the [explicative] Mexican piss out of you, homey." The officer then kicks the man's hand and face. A female officer then walks over and steps on the man's leg. Ultimately, after the police learn he is not one of the suspects they were looking for, the man is helped up and let go. The officer has apologized, but we learned as children that there are some behaviors for which saying you are sorry is not the end of it. A most disturbing element in this particular incident is that, as happens in most videos, other officers are present and take no action. A criminal investigation is underway at this time.

Whenever these tapes are shown, as happened with the Rodney King incident, some police officers, police executives, representatives of police associations, and other "talking head" police "experts" say that the actions of the officer/s involved may be justified. Civil rights groups point to the videotapes and cry racism and some say that they show that all police are brutal. It is hard for the officers involved in these incidents to convince a skeptical public and community that the level of force could be justified. On the other hand, it is hard to support the allegation that all or a majority of the police are brutal. The evidence is not there. Nevertheless, it is disturbing that many believe it is.

All of the above incidents serve to point out that we still have an ethical crisis in law enforcement. There is reason to believe that we have always had an ethical crisis in law enforcement and may always have one. The reason lies in the nature of the occupation.

A MORALLY DANGEROUS OCCUPATION

In 1829, with the Metropolitan Police Act, the publicly paid watchman, voluntary watches, and paid police in the London area were centralized under the national government and became members of a new occupation that would spread throughout England and Wales, and reach the shores of the Colonies that were to become America. It was immediately recognized that the members of the new police occupation should be held to a higher standard of integrity than the average citizen. However, the original London Metropolitan Police were not of high moral caliber. Many were often accused of being drunk on duty and associating in public houses with prostitutes and suspicious persons. In the first two years, more than 3,200 constables left the new police occupation, more than two-thirds dismissed for drunkenness (Ascoli, 1979: 89). There is evidence that some of the Metro officers accepted payoffs from illegal gambling dens and brothels (Reynolds, 1998: 153; Miller, 1997: 28–29).

The nature of the duties: close contact with the public, control of vice activities, discretion, and low visibility decision making; combined with the enormous power inherent in the office, made this new occupation a morally dangerous occupation for its members. This became painfully clear when the new model of policing was transported to America where local control of police agencies was constitutionally mandated (Miller, 1997; Lane, 1971). The early American experience demonstrated that the police could become not only corrupt but the instruments and servants of local politicians. Community control run amok is an apt description of the American police at the time (Walker, 1977). The early American police in their crime-fighting duties became a greater threat to a free society than corrupt police officers and led to a series of reform movements that continues today (Fogelson, 1977). Since the creation of the new occupation – law enforcement – all police organizations, particularly those in free societies, have had to deal with three perennial problems: Abuse of Authority (unnecessary use of force and Noble Cause Injustice), Corruption, and Dealings with Minorities (discrimination and racial and ethnic profiling).

BLESSING OR CURSE

The early framers of the new occupation and what were to become the modern-day police organizations in Great Britain and the United States recognized that a paid public police agency could become a blessing or a curse in a democracy (Lee, 1971: xxxi). That is, the police could be the defenders of liberty or the oppressors of a free people. The early framers recognized the possibility of Noble Cause Injustice. Prevention of crime and the maintenance of order (noble end) by oppressive and undemocratic means could become more intolerable than the effects of crime or disorder. Whatever justice is applied in a free society begins and sometimes ends with the first decision makers – the police. Lee stated that the ideal police force is one that grants the maximum protection with the minimum interference in the lives of the people:

> Government cannot be exercised without coercion, but the coercion employed ought to be reduced to the lowest possible limit consistent with safety, the ideal police force being one which affords the maximum of protection at the cost of a minimum of interference with the lawful liberty of the subject. (Lee, 1971: xxx)

The constitutional and legal restraints on American police officers exist to limit the coercive intrusions of the police into the personal lives of American citizens. The Common Law, court decisions and acts of Parliament exist to limit the coercive intrusions of police into the personal lives of British citizens (Robilliard & McEwan, 1986). However, modern-day police forces in Great Britain and the United States are expanding their coercive "interference" into the lives of their citizens under the evangelistic rhetoric of Community Policing. Ultimately, the complex questions involved in police discretionary decisions, particularly extra-legal practices, as the police deal with "quality of life" crimes/problems of disorder, will be decided in the courts of both countries (Livingstone, 1997). Brogdon (1999: 181) states that "community policing is only possible when the constitutional rights of citizens are vague rather than distinct, and especially where the police mandate is permissive rather than restrictive – conditions that do not exist in Great Britain or the United States." Whether or not this "expansion of coercive interference" will be a revolutionary new police reform or another politically motivated (and federally financed) police management fad that passes into history remains to be seen.

NEED FOR ETHICAL BEHAVIOR

The American police as individuals, groups, and organizations have been both a blessing and a curse. Admittedly, the list of blessings is voluminous. However, the litany and horrors and abuse in the 1990s include Rodney King, Malice Green, Abner Louima, Amadou Diallo, Michael Dowd, Waco, Ruby Ridge, Ramparts, Mark Furman, Antoinette Frank, and Len Davis. Thus far in the twenty-first century we have Sean Bell; the NYPD Mafia Cops (Stephen Caracappa & Louis Eppolito); Chicago PD Officer, Joseph Miedzianowski; corrupt FBI agents John Connolly and H. Paul Ricco; FBI spies Robert Hanssen and Earl Edwin Pitts; and the Los Angeles Immigration Rally. One hears terms associated with the police, like racial profiling, positional asphyxia deaths, chokeholds, whoops raids, "testilying." In recent years, in addition to corruption scandals in New York City, Philadelphia, Chicago, Cleveland, Los Angeles, New Orleans, Miami, Detroit, and Atlanta, cases and convictions have been dismissed because police officers planted evidence or lied in reports, warrants, and in court. The unethical behavior of those working in this *morally dangerous occupation* receives more attention and is easier to measure than the good, or ethical behavior, or at least that is the way it appears from examining the media (*Adam 12* was never as popular as *NYPD Blue*) and the literature, particularly the scholarly literature. This is inevitable because of the basic nature of policing.

The ethical behavior of police officers in any democracy (Great Britain, the United States, or any free state) is central to police work because of the nature of policing. Policing is forceful, or potentially forceful, social control no matter what label is attached to it (Professional Policing, Community Service Policing, Community-Oriented Policing, Order Maintenance Policing, Zero Tolerance Policing, and whatever comes next). That is the way it has always been and will always be. The use of force, or potential use of force, has been used by every community in history as a means to secure the effective observance of laws (Reith, 1952). Given the inherent coercive nature of police work and moral risk it poses for its workers, a commitment to ethical conduct is a must. A small number of deviant individuals are attracted to police work for the numerous opportunities to continue their abhorrent conduct and sometimes find support among misguided colleagues who will not report them. Ethical conduct is ultimately what protects the citizens of a free society from the police. Ethical behavior is necessary if the occupation is to ever become a profession, even though some argue that it is now.

IS LAW ENFORCEMENT A PROFESSION?

If we were to accept the word of law enforcement spokespersons and read the "professional" law enforcement literature, the answer to this question would be an emphatic yes! The International Association of Chiefs of Police (IACP), the professional voice of law enforcement, unequivocally states that law enforcement is a profession that:

- Is dedicated to the service of others.
- Requires personal commitment to service beyond the normal eight-hour day.
- Requires of its practitioners specialized knowledge and skills.
- Governs itself in relation to standards of admission, training and performance.
- Has mechanisms to ensure conformance and a disciplinary system to punish deviations.
- Forms associations to improve their collective ability to enhance service to others.
- Is guided by a code of ethics. (IACP, 1981)

I certainly agree with some of the IACP statements cited above, such as dedicated to the service of others, requires personal commitment beyond an eight-hour day, requires specialized skills and knowledge, and forms associations. I could mount a strong argument against the statement that law enforcement "governs itself in relation to standards of admission, training and performance." The standards for admission range from "minimum" [I have always hated the use of this term in relation to police admission standards] standards of 21, high school graduation or G.E.D., a driver's license, and no serious criminal record in some states to a baccalaureate degree at the federal level for special agent positions. The wide differences between training and performance standards among American Law Enforcement agencies are well known to all.

Does the law enforcement "profession" have "mechanisms to ensure conformance and a disciplinary system to punish deviations?" Some agencies do and some agencies don't. The mechanisms and systems work in some agencies but not in others. Some states have a system to certify law enforcement officers but no system to decertify them. We certainly do not have a profession-wide system similar to the American Bar Association or the American Medical Association. The statement that the law enforcement "profession" "is guided by a code of ethics" will be addressed later. Whether or not one agrees that law enforcement is a profession, one has to agree that law enforcement, as a morally dangerous occupation, has come a long way since the establishment of the London Metropolitan Police in 1829. Furthermore, law enforcement in the United States has made tremendous strides since its transplant to New York City in 1845.

Actually, the debate over whether or not law enforcement is a profession is best left to those who have the patience and time to argue theoretical and philosophical issues. I have neither. I thoroughly agree with FBI Special Agent Donald Witham, that "reasonable and intelligent people could argue endlessly as to whether or not law enforcement meets all the characteristics of a profession" (Witham, 1985: 30). However, I also agree with Witham that as a practical matter, no American occupational group has ever succeeded in having itself accepted as a profession without requiring the minimum educational standard of a baccalaureate degree (Witham, 1985: 34).

I do not advocate that we give up on the law enforcement profession as a goal. It has been the goal of many police reformers and reform movements since the early 1900s, but "saying it is so ain't going to make it so." The goal may not have been realized, but there has been progress and it is still worth striving for. This led us to the really important question – Can law enforcement officers be professional?

CAN LAW ENFORCEMENT OFFICERS BE PROFESSIONAL?

If we can agree that the term professional is an adjective and refers to *behavior*, the answer to this question is an emphatic and unequivocal – yes! That is, yes; if law enforcement officers know what they are doing, are proud of what they are doing, and if they prescribe to and follow a code of ethical behavior. At this time, we rely on the preservice and in-service training curriculums of the various law enforcement agencies at the local, state, and federal levels to ensure that law enforcement officers know what they are doing. To a degree, these same training centers or academies create a sense of pride in their trainees. This sense of pride is also dependent on the manner in which individual officers, groups of officers, and the occupation, as a whole, prescribe to and follow a code of ethical behavior.

Chapter 2

PROFESSIONAL/OCCUPATIONAL ETHICS

INTRODUCTION

Morality refers to the standards of behavior that should be followed by everyone. Ethics is concerned with how individuals should conduct themselves (Heffernan, 1997: 25). Dan Carlson, associate director of the Southwestern Law Enforcement Institute, states that one way of defining ethics is "Doing the right thing, when nobody will know if you do the wrong thing" (http://web2airmail. net/slf/summer95/tick.html). Professional/occupational ethics deals with behavior that all members of a professional occupational group should adhere to because they are members of the group (Davis, 1997: 37). This is practical ethics concerned with how members of the effected group solve practical problems (Kamm, 1997: 123).

Professional/occupational ethical standards are contained in the Codes of Ethics adopted by the occupational group. Codes of Ethics are put forward as public evidence of a "determination, on the part of the providers themselves, to serve in ways that are predictable and acceptable" (Kleinig, 1997: 242). The purpose of a code of ethics is to establish formal guidelines for ethical behavior and eliminate the ambiguity that surrounds individual considerations of what is right and wrong behavior (U.S. Department of Justice, 1978: 18–22). Codes are no substitute for good character and wisdom; however, they can serve as a general guideline for the groups' behavior (Delattre, 1989: 32). The ethical principles are in effect the occupation's recognition of guidelines for action.

POLICE CODES OF ETHICS

There was a Code of Ethics embedded in the standards for the London Metropolitan Police in 1829. However, it wasn't until 1928 that a Code of Ethics was developed for the United States police (Kleinig, 1996: 235). The current version appears below and will be discussed in detail later:

LAW ENFORCEMENT CODE OF ETHICS*

As a law enforcement officer, my fundamental duty is to serve the community; to safeguard lives and property; to protect the innocent against deception, the weak against oppression or intimidation and the peaceful against violence or disorder; and to respect the Constitutional rights of all to liberty, equality and justice.

I will keep my private life unsullied as an example to all and will behave in a manner that does not bring discredit to me or my agency. I will maintain courageous calm in the face of danger, scorn or ridicule; develop self-restraint; and be constantly mindful of the welfare of others. Honest in thought and deed both in my personal and official life, I will be exemplary in obeying the law and the regulations of my department. Whatever I hear of a confidential nature or that is confided to me in my official capacity will be kept ever secret unless revelation is necessary in the performance of my duty.

I will never act officiously or permit personal feelings, prejudices, political beliefs, aspirations, animosities or friendships to influence my decisions. With no compromise for crime and with relentless prosecution of criminals, I will enforce the law courteously and appropriately without fear or favor, malice or ill will, never employing unnecessary force or violence and never accepting gratuities.

I recognize the badge of my office as a symbol of public faith, and I accept it as a public trust to be held so long as I am true to the ethics of police service. I will never engage in acts of corruption or bribery, nor will I condone such acts by other police officers. I will cooperate with all legally authorized agencies and their representatives in the pursuit of justice.

I know that I alone am responsible for my own standard of professional performance and will take every reasonable opportunity to enhance and improve my level of knowledge and competence.

---

*Source: www.theiacp.org/publinfo/Pubs/CodeofEthic.htm.

I will constantly strive to achieve these objectives and ideals, dedicating myself before God to my chosen profession . . . law enforcement.

The International Association of Chiefs of Police

In addition, the IACP, at its 107th Annual Conference in San Diego, California, passed a resolution adopting the Law Enforcement Oath of Honor submitted by the association's Police Image and Ethics Committee.

LAW ENFORCEMENT OATH OF HONOR

*On my honor,
I will never betray my badge,
my integrity, my character,
or the public trust.
I will always have
the courage to hold myself
and others accountable for our actions.
I will always uphold the constitution
and community I serve.*

The IACP advocates that all officers take this short oath and that it be recited at "assembled public and internal gatherings of law enforcement officers (public ceremonies, promotional events, law enforcement conferences, etc.); placed on signs and conspicuously displayed throughout law enforcement facilities; printed on the back of business cards and other types of agency materials; incorporated at every opportunity in policies, procedures, and training materials; referred to by administrators in conversation and correspondence; and referenced in both positive and negative personnel actions" (http://www.theiacp.org/profassist/ethics/focus_on_ethics.htm). In other words, the Law Enforcement Oath of Honor should get the maximum exposure in all police organizations and functions. This will serve to heighten the awareness and visibility of ethical standards embodied in the Law Enforcement Code of Ethics.

There is also a Statement of Ethical Principles for police officers in England, Wales, and Northern Ireland (Haggard, 1994: 2–3).

STATEMENT OF ETHICAL PRINCIPLES

(England, Wales, and Northern Ireland)

I will act with fairness, carrying out responsibilities with integrity and impartiality;

Perform duties with diligence and the proper use of discretion;

In dealings with all individuals, both outside and inside the police service, display self control, tolerance, understanding and courtesy appropriate to the circumstances;

Uphold fundamental human rights, treating every person as an individual and display respect and compassion towards them;

Support all colleagues in the performance of their lawful duties and in doing so, actively oppose and draw attention to any malpractice by any person;

Respect the fact that much of the information I receive is confidential and may only be divulged when my duty requires me to do so;

Exercise force when justified and use only the minimum amount of force to affect my lawful purpose and restore the peace;

Use resources entrusted to me to the maximum benefit of the public;

Act only within the law, in the understanding that I have no authority to depart from due legal process and that no one may place a requirement on me to do so;

Continually accept responsibility for self-development, continually seeking to improve the way in which I serve the community;

Accept personal responsibility for my own acts and omissions.

The interest in Codes of Ethics governing police behavior is growing worldwide. The second principle of democratic policing drafted for the United Nations Police Task Force in Sarajevo-Herzgovina stated that the police as recipients of public trust should be governed by a code of professional conduct (Travis, 1998: 3). Furthermore, this code should reflect the highest ethical values that could provide the basis for identifying acts of misconduct. On June 10 and 11, 1996, the Council of Europe, a thirty-nine-member organization, met in Strasbourg, France. The topic of their meeting was police ethics and a code of conduct for European police officers (McDonald, Gaffigan & Greenberg, 1997: 81).

CONCLUSION

As stated earlier, morality refers to the standards of behavior all should follow; ethics is concerned with how individuals conduct themselves. A moral police officer just like any moral person would not steal, murder, or rape. But we expect more from police officers, they are to conduct themselves according to Professional/Occupational ethical standards. And, acting ethically or unethically is ultimately an individual choice. Therefore, we are left with the question – Do Codes of Conduct provide police officers with the guidance to make ethical choices? An examination of the IACP Law Enforcement Code of Ethics may provide an answer.

Chapter 3

LAW ENFORCEMENT CODE OF ETHICS – PARAGRAPH 1

AS A LAW ENFORCEMENT OFFICER, my fundamental duty is to serve mankind; to safeguard lives and property; to protect the innocent against deception, the weak against oppression or intimidation, and the peaceful against violation or disorder; and to respect the Constitutional rights of all men to liberty, equality and justice.

The **Law Enforcement Code of Ethics** begins with a series of ideal statements that may be hard for most mortals to live up to. They sound like something William Wallace, the Scottish hero of the movie **Brave Heart**, might have said. Should they be disregarded as guides for police ethical behavior? Do these ideal statements have any practical use for law enforcement? The answer to the first question is an emphatic *no* and the answer to the second question is an equally emphatic *yes*.

Before we begin our discussion, we should first define law enforcement officer, in order to identify those who we believe are subject to the standards and rules of conduct contained in the **Code**. A law enforcement officer is any **public official**, who has the **extraordinary powers of arrest**, and they or their agency performs at least one of the three **direct police services** of patrol, traffic control, or criminal investigation (Barker, Hunter & Rush, 1994).

The term **public official** should not need any further definition. The **Code** applies only to public police who perform a service and not to private police who operate for the profit motive. The term **extraordinary power of arrest refers** to those arrest powers granted by statute to public officials. We are referring to arrest powers that are above and beyond those possessed by citizens in a democracy. Technically, all citizens in a democracy have citizen arrest powers. However, they are more limited and restricted than those granted to public officials who are paid to do full time what is essentially every citizen's responsibility.

The third element in our definition of law enforcement officer is that the agency or the officer performs one of the three **direct police services** of patrol, traffic control, and criminal investigation.

> **Patrol** – is the organized surveillance of public places within a specified territory and response to reports of suspected criminal acts for the purpose of preventing crime, apprehending offenders, or maintaining public order. Officers on patrol also frequently respond to calls that are not crime related.
> **Traffic Control** – includes monitoring vehicular traffic and investigation of traffic accidents.
> **Criminal Investigation** – is activity undertaken to identify alleged criminals, to gather evidence for criminal proceedings or to recover stolen goods. (Ostrom, Parks & Whitaker, 1978: 24)

The definition does not imply that the agency or the officers must perform all three direct police services. Very few agencies above the local/municipal level would perform all three. However, they or their agency must perform one of the three. State Highway Patrol officers might only perform traffic control with a separate state agency responsible for criminal investigation, but they both would be law enforcement officers. The nonuniformed special agents for numerous criminal investigation agencies at all levels of government are all law enforcement officers. Some of the security officers for the Smithsonian Institution's Office of Protective Services perform patrol activities, often at fixed points in the museums. Others engage in only criminal investigation duties and still others perform traffic control duties. They are all by our definition law enforcement officers and subject to the **Code**.

Having defined those subject to the **Law Enforcement Code of Ethics**, we can now redirect our attention to the first paragraph. The three key concepts in this paragraph are *service*, *protect*, and *respect*. To serve and protect are familiar terms to the police. They are usually emblazoned on marked police vehicles. Countless number of police officers has sacrificed their lives in an effort to serve and protect the public.

As stated above, the law enforcement officer is first and foremost a public official. He or she works for some governmental entity whether at the local, county, state, or federal level. As public officials, they have sworn an oath to serve and protect their clientele whether it be the visitors to the Smithsonian museums, the students on the campus of Eastern Kentucky University, the citizens of New York City, or the citizens of the United States as in the case of the Federal Bureau of Investigation.

Walker (1983) stated that the three dominant features of policing could be traced back to our English heritage. They are:

1. **Limited authority** – the powers of the police are closely circumscribed by law. As mentioned above, individual liberty is jealously protected at the expense of crime control.
2. **Local control** – The responsibility for providing police services rests primarily in local governments. While there are numerous variations within the United States regarding the organization of local, state, and federal law enforcement agencies, for the most part policing in the United States is highly decentralized and found in local agencies.
3. **Fragmented law enforcement** – The responsibility for providing police services, which is borne predominately by local agencies, is usually divided among several different agencies within an area. This often leads to problems with communication, cooperation and control among the agencies.

These features were incorporated into policing to protect citizens from the abuse of a strong state or federal government.

The law enforcement officer at any level of government is but one group of public officials that comprises our nation's formal means of social control – the Criminal Justice System. This system exists to accomplish four purposes: (1) control and prevent crime, (2) punish offenders, (3) treat and reform those amenable to such treatment, and (4) incapacitate those not amenable for treatment.

Law enforcement officers are in a sense the "gatekeepers" of this criminal justice system or process, if you will. Their outputs are the inputs to the other subsystems of the criminal justice system. They learn about crime from citizens, by discovery from officers in the field, or through investigation and intelligence efforts. Once they verify that a crime has occurred, they must identify a suspect and, if possible, apprehend him or her for the criminal justice process to proceed (Barker, Hunter & Rush, 1994: 22). However, if we examine the first paragraph of the **Code**, we see that there is no specific mention of crime, crime prevention, making arrests, investigation, writing citations, running traffic, or even the criminal justice system. That is because the police in a democracy while performing their crime related duties have a higher calling or purpose.

The last sentence in the first paragraph of the **Code** "to respect the Constitutional rights of all men to liberty, equality and justice" is the essence of the law enforcement mission in a free society such as ours. The National Advisory Commission on Criminal Justice Standards and Goals, in their report on the police, stated, "If the overall purpose of the police service in America were narrowed to a single objective, that objective would be **to preserve the peace in a manner consistent with the freedoms secured by the Constitution**" (National Advisory Commission on Criminal Justice Standards and Goals, 1973: 13).

Law enforcement officers in a democratic society represent the most important protectors of individual and group liberties. They are vested with a significant amount of authority to restrict the free movement of persons and to lawfully subject citizens to embarrassment or indignity in the course of the investigation, search, and/or arrest process (Barker & Carter, 1994). They have the right to use coercive force up to and including deadly force to affect these duties. Therefore, the misuse of their authority can and often does represent the greatest threat to the individual and group liberties they are to protect.

The police in a free society such as ours have a hard task to perform. They must perform their duties and exercise their authority within the constraints of the law. All actions they take are subject to review for their legality. The familiar names of **Mapp**, **Miranda**, **Escobedo**, and **Schmerber** represent Supreme Court decisions that restricted police actions in dealing with citizens. Although recent Supreme Court decisions, such as *Terry v. Ohio*, *U.S. v Leon*, *Chimel v. California*, *Hester v. U.S.* to name a few, may have relaxed some restrictions on law enforcement behavior; they were also decided on Constitutional and not crime control issues.

The fear of governmental abuse and zealous protection of civil liberties and individual rights embodied in our Constitution and the Bill of Rights will always interfere with the crime control efforts of law enforcement agencies. However, that is the way our forefathers and countless generations of Americans wanted it. We are willing to tolerate greater amounts of crime and criminality to protect our individual freedoms. We, as a free society, will not tolerate a law enforcement agency staffed by **Dirty Harry's**, who use illegal and unethical means to accomplish what they perceive as legitimate ends. We will always closely examine the means to which the ends of law enforcement were accomplished. Furthermore, we will always depend on law enforcement officers who prescribe to the **Law Enforcement Code of Ethics** to "respect the Constitutional rights of all men to liberty, equality and justice."

Chapter 4

LAW ENFORCEMENT CODE OF ETHICS – PARAGRAPH 2

I WILL keep my private life unsullied as an example to all and will behave in a manner that does not bring discredit to me or my agency. I will maintain courageous calm in the face of danger, scorn or ridicule; develop self restraint; and be constantly mindful of the welfare of others. Honest in thought and deed both in my personal and official life, I will be exemplary in obeying the law and the regulations of my department. Whatever I hear of a confidential nature or that is confided to me in my official capacity will be kept ever secret unless revelation is necessary in the performance of my duty.

In this paragraph, there are two references to an officer's private life; "I will keep my private life unsullied as an example to all, honest in thought and deed in both my personal and official life." Should an officer's private life be subject to review and scrutiny? Before we answer that question, we should consider that law enforcement officer, special agent or cop, if you will, is an example of what is known as a master status.

A status is the social position we occupy in a group. And, we all occupy several social positions in various groups. For example, I occupy the social positions of college professor, police academy instructor, expert witness, husband, father, etc. A master status is one that cuts across all the statuses you may hold and comes to be the one that you are known by and, often, the standard that identifies your expected behavior. As you can imagine, the master status that most often is used to describe me is college professor. A master status often literally takes over and controls one's identity. It conjures up a mental image for most people and its "wearer" is always judged in relation to it.

Some master statuses once held are held for life. The bearer only becomes an "ex, e.g.," ex-marine, ex-cop, ex-con, ex-pro in sports, ex-prizefighter, etc. Consider how many times Lee Harvey Oswald and Charles Whitman, the latter the mass murderer in the bell tower at the University of Texas at Austin, were referred to, and are still being referred to as Ex-Marines. Yet, neither of these two assassins spent more than a short tour in the Marine Corps. Tony Danza, the actor, is still being referred to as an ex-prizefighter although he had a modest 13–3 record many years ago. If a person goes to the penitentiary, no matter how long they live, they will be known as ex-cons. The same applies to cops. After you are no longer a cop, you will simply become an ex-cop for life. Timothy J. Poole was sentenced to 400 months in federal court for mail and wire fraud charges in connection with a August 1, 2006 double murder of his adoptive mother and stepfather. The banner headline of the Department of Justice Press Release reads: *Former Florence County Deputy Sentenced to 400 Years' Imprisonment* (DOJ 2010). The write-up states, "Poole served as a deputy with the Florence County Sheriff's Office from 1997 to 2002." He left police work four years before the murders occurred, yet he is still identified as former deputy sheriff, even by law enforcement sources.

Given that your cop master status defines your identity and is used as the standard to judge the appropriateness or inappropriateness of your behavior, we should return to our question concerning a law enforcement officer's personal life. Should it be subject to review and scrutiny? Actually, the answer to that question is really academic. Whether or not it should or should not be, it is subject to review and scrutiny by the public because law enforcement is a master status. Therefore, the law enforcement officer should strive to keep his or her private life unsullied as an example to all. Any off-duty behavior that can have on-duty consequences is subject to review and scrutiny. The officer who is known to drink excessively, gamble, or not pay his debts will be judged more harshly by those who know him or her. If he or she is known to be a liar, his or her court testimony will be held in question. Being caught in a lie related to official duties will affect the officer's credibility and make him or her useless as a courtroom witness. If the officer is known to be abusive to his or her family members, those who know him or her will always wonder how he or she can impartially handle domestic disturbances on the job. Those who know that he or she arrests nonpolice for the same offense will view the officer who drinks and drives as a hypocrite.

Behavior that calls into question officers' rational decision-making processes will get them fired. For example, a North Carolina State Trooper was fired for trapping and then shooting a neighbor's five-month-old kitten. The trooper's excuse was the kitten was climbing on his cars (Biesecker, 2010). A Midland County, Texas deputy was fired and three others suspended for taking the picture of a scantily clad waitress sitting on their marked police vehicle with one of the officer's assault weapons. Two female Wisconsin sheriff's deputies took pictures of a dummy propped against a burning cross wearing a department uniform, while saying that "the burning cross has a KKK aspect to it." The deputies posted a video of the incident on Facebook. One deputy resigned and the other a sergeant was demoted to dispatcher.

Repercussions' for certain offenses cannot be avoided; once the officer pins on the badge and takes the oath, his or her private life comes under the microscope. Drunk driving arrests will get an officer suspended or fired in most police departments. In North Carolina, an officer's off-duty DUI and failure to arrest got three officers fired. A Butner, North Carolina police officer stopped a North Carolina Highway Patrol captain for DWI and called for a supervisor (APd, May 13, 2010). The two Butner officers, a captain and a lieutenant took the Highway Patrol captain to a motel instead of jail after consulting with an off-duty Butner police major who was awakened. After the incident became known, the two Butner officers and the Highway Patrol captain were fired and the Butner major suspended without pay while an internal investigation was being conducted. The major was later fired. In Tecumseh, Michigan, three officers were disciplined for stopping a deputy sheriff for drunken driving and taking him home instead of arresting him (Frownfelder, 2010). The deputy convinced his daughter to take him back to his vehicle that he drove off and wrecked. He was arrested and subsequently fired. Domestic violence convictions will result in termination and sometimes prison sentences. A Jersey City police officer was sentenced to five years in prison for assaulting the mother of his 15-month-child and leaving the child at home alone while he searched for the woman who did not come home from work on time (Conte, May 1, 2010). Police officers can be fired for violating protection orders. A Schenectady, New York police officer was fired and sentenced to three years probation for text messaging his former girlfriend, a county corrections officer (Stanforth, 2010). The text messages violated a protection order. The arrest and conviction for most misdemeanors, especially those involving moral turpitude, and all felonies will result in termination.

A Cape Coral, Florida officer was fired when Key West, Florida officers found marijuana in his rented vacation home while investigating a shots fired call. The officer was originally charged with possession. The charge was dismissed after it was determined that the marijuana belonged to his wife. The officer was actually fired for conduct unbecoming an officer for not taking some action to address his wife's illegal behavior.

Police officers have committed heinous crimes off-duty that have nothing to do with their occupational duties. They are criminals or sexual deviant/predators who happen to carry a badge. A 20-year veteran Hawaii deputy sheriff pleaded guilty to molesting his niece starting when the child was in the first grade and continuing for four years (Sugimoto, 2010). Under his plea agreement, the former deputy avoided a ten-year sentence and was sentenced to a year in jail and five years probation. What would an average citizen have received for the same crime? A Tacoma, Washington police officer was charged with sexually molesting a female relative from 1996 to 2003 (Mulick, 2010). The alleged molestation started when the victim was five or six and continued until she was 12. A Philadelphia police officer was charged with sexually assaulting three girls, two of them relatives, from 1991 to 2000 (Dale, 2010). The sexual assaults started when the girls were under 14. One victim alleged that the abuse started when she was 11 and continued until she was 18. The officer was charged with 500 sex-offense counts, including rape, incest, statutory sexual assault, and endangering the welfare of children in his care. A Mesa, Arizona police officer was convicted of 32 counts of child molestation, sexual exploitation of a minor, and furnishing obscene materials to a minor (Collom, 2010). The victims were a 10-year-old boy and a nine-year-old girl and the incidents took place in his house.

The next cases demonstrate that there is no cure for stupidity when sex is involved. A 23-year veteran lieutenant with the California Highway Patrol was one of 12 sexual perverts caught in a sting arranged by local police and Perverted-Justice.com (Welborn, 2009). Perverted-Justice.com is a nonprofit group that targets pedophiles and has as its mission protecting children from Internet sexual predators. The lieutenant was allowed to retire after his arrest. He was convicted but received probation instead of prison time, stunning the prosecutor and the courtroom. An eight-year veteran of the Bibb County, Georgia Sheriff's Department was caught in an FBI sting soliciting sex with a seven-year-old girl (DOJ, 2010). He received a sentence of 20 years in a federal prison. A San Antonio police officer pleaded no contest to exposing himself to a college student while off-duty (Kapitan, 2010). A surveillance video caught him speeding away from the school's parking lot. A Monroe County, Florida deputy sheriff was fired for providing alcohol to a 15-year-old boy then showing him pornographic movies and fondling him (Hatzipanagos, 2010).

Law enforcement officers at all levels commit crimes while off duty unconnected to their police duties. An FBI special agent in Nashville, Tennessee was indicted by a federal grand jury for 19 counts, including wire fraud and bank fraud in a scheme to rip off a mortgage company (Carey, 2010). According to the indictment, the FBI special agent lied about his profession and income to get financing to buy rental properties in 2006. He is also accused of lying about his income and assets during a 2009 personal bankruptcy proceeding. A Warrensville Heights, Ohio police officer was charged with operating a Ponzi scheme that targeted the law enforcement community (DOJ, June 3, 2010). He defrauded 25 investors, including active and retired police officers and firefighters, of approximately $889,000.

The **Code** says that a law enforcement officer should be honest in thought and deed. However, it is just a part of life that we as humans will not at times be honest or moral in thought. As long as these thoughts do not become an obsession or translate into action, it is probably normal. However, we should not budge an inch from demanding that all law enforcement officers are honest in deed both in their personal and official life. Integrity is just too important to being a professional law enforcement officer that it cannot be compromised in either the officer's personal or official life.

Officers are expected to be "exemplary in obeying the law and the regulation of the department." That includes not flaunting one's position as a law enforcement officer. A Massachusetts state trooper parked in a handicapped parking spot in front of a Dunkin Donuts in Framingham, Massachusetts to place his order. When a citizen asked him, while holding a recorder, why he was breaking the law, the angry trooper threatened to arrest the citizen (Curran, 2010).

Maintaining calm in the face of danger, scorn, or ridicule and developing self-restraint are noble principles to ascribe to. The overwhelming majority of law enforcement officers in this country adhere to these principles. One only has to compare the police handling of anti-everything incidents from abortion to gay rights demonstrations and protests in recent years to what was common during the "police riots" of the sixties.

Obviously, we would expect that law enforcement officers would obey the laws of the land and the regulation of their department. We would also expect that confidential information that comes to the officer by way of his or her official position would be kept secret. Friends, acquaintances, and even relatives sometimes ask law enforcement officers for information on cases or people who have been arrested. The majority of the time the officer being questioned will know nothing about the case or the person. Citizens do not seem to understand that they may have more information from media sources than the officer has. However, on occasion, the officer may be privy to the requested information. It should be kept confidential. Most people understand that those who tell secrets cannot be trusted to keep secrets. The officer who gossips or reveals confidential information will soon acquire the reputation of being untrustworthy.

Chapter 5

LAW ENFORCEMENT CODE OF ETHICS – PARAGRAPH 3

I WILL never act officiously or permit personal feelings, prejudices, political beliefs, aspirations, animosities or friendships to influence my decisions. With no compromise for crime and with relentless prosecution of criminals, I will enforce the law courteously and appropriately without fear or favor, malice or ill will, never employing unnecessary force or violence and never accepting gratuities.

The first sentence of this paragraph makes clear that law enforcement officers who prescribe to the **Code** should always remember they are not the law; they are only paid full time to enforce the law. Their duties should never become personal. The "avenging angel syndrome" where officers exact their sense of street justice on individuals and groups they personally dislike is to be avoided at all costs. We expect law enforcement officers to be even-handed in the execution of their duties. However, all law enforcement officers are human beings and because of that, they will have personal feelings. They will have buttons that if pushed will make them mad. It is often said that most people go to jail or get citations for "contempt of cop" – COC. Not showing the proper respect or challenging the officer's authority will get you in jail or a ticket according to this concept. The professional law enforcement officer will rise above the need to ensure respect through his or her arrest powers. His or her discretionary powers should not be exercised for personal reasons no matter how strong.

The law enforcement officer can, and does, exercise a tremendous amount of discretion and, particularly for nonserious misdemeanors or traffic citations, there is no need to put everyone in jail who violates the law or give a ticket to everyone who commits a traffic infraction. There are numerous situations where warnings, counseling, or a word of advice are a better choice of action than arrest or citation. Chiefs and sheriffs are continually reminding me that police academies do a good job of telling "rookies" when to make an arrest. However, the academies often fail at telling police officers when not to make an arrest. Conversations with current academy instructors tell me that this is changing as current instruction moves to a more problem-solving orientation. Modern law enforcement professionals recognize that arrest is not always the best way to solve a problem.

The rigid personality who feels that he or she must enforce all criminal and traffic violations will never become a true professional law enforcement officer. Those officers who proudly announce that they would give their own wife or mother a ticket if they saw them break a traffic law are either liars or fools, maybe both. They are also not the officers we want answering domestic disturbance calls or handling protests or, for that matter, any police action that requires tact and judgment. In this country, selective enforcement of traffic laws is the norm. Selective enforcement is the only practical approach to traffic enforcement. Full enforcement of the law, particularly traffic laws, is not logical, practical, or wanted by the citizens. The officer must adhere to the principle of reasonableness in making his or her decisions. They must consider the total situation and what is the end they want to attain with their action. I remember years ago working a major college football game when my young partner asked if we were going to arrest all the drunks. I told him that I didn't know where we would put them all. The city jail would not hold them. I also told him that I thought the city would have to call in the National Guard to handle the ensuing riot. We did make some arrests that day, but we certainly did not arrest all the drunks in the football stadium. I could recite other instances where officers I worked with did not arrest or ticket someone who broke the law or a traffic regulation, but that is not necessary. Every working law enforcement officer can recite numerous instances from his or her own experiences.

We will discuss the issue of unnecessary use of force fully later. However, we should all recognize at this time that the unnecessary use of force by police officers is certainly not consistent with our definition of a professional law enforcement officer.

The **Code** is very explicit on the acceptance of gratuities. It says: law enforcement officers **will** never accept gratuities. It does not say those over a certain monetary amount. It does not indicate if there is a difference between systematic and incidental gratuities. The **Code** does not mention the intent of the giver or the effect on the officer's behavior. There is no mention of the acceptance of gratuities as a possible "grey area" of corruption. These questions will all be addressed more fully later. Two issues that I will raise at this time are the effect of police acceptance of gratuities, no matter how small, on those who observe officers in uniform receiving free cups of coffee or discount meals and how those who give these favors to the police may view it.

Those having to pay for their coffee and full price for their meals may not hold a very high opinion of their public servants receiving free coffee and discounted meals. They probably will not be sympathetic to police demands for pay raises and increased benefits. I have often heard the following comment from citizens and even council members who were in the position of voting on police pay raises: "Why should we give the police more money, they get everything they want free or discounted now?" It is hard to argue against this statement in an area where it is well known that the giving and accepting of small and large gratuities by law enforcement officers is common practice. Some are even more animate in their description of their public servants when they refer to them as "free loading sons of bitches."

Now, lets examine the perception of those who give these favors to the police. When discussing this issue in training sessions, I always relate the following personal experience. While working in plain clothes, I stopped in a well-known fast food restaurant; the identity will remain anonymous, but I guarantee you there is one or more in every city I have been in and they are well-known for giving police free or discounted meals and drinks. It was closing time when I ordered my Coke and cheeseburger. While waiting at the counter for my order, I observed the following. There was a tray of unsold and unwrapped hamburgers and cheeseburgers lying on the table in the back. One of the young high school-aged workers picked up the tray and emptied it in the garbage. The manager on seeing her do this screamed, "Don't throw them away – we always give them to the precinct." At this point, the manager and the young worker picked the hamburgers and cheeseburgers out of the garbage and wrapped them and put them in a large carryout sack. A few seconds later a smiling uniformed officer came in and was given the sack. The manager smiled and told him, "Tell the guys to enjoy." I followed the police car to the precinct and was able to tell the hungry officers what had happened before they ate the filthy meal. It then took me about 15 minutes to talk them out of going back there and putting the manager in jail. I told them that the publicity would make them look bad and probably give other restaurant owners some bad ideas. The last comment convinced them to cease and detest. However, I can only imagine what may have happened to the manager and the restaurant later.

Thus far we have discussed gratuities as if they were only gifts and favors given to patrol officers during their routine duties; nothing could be farther from the truth. Gifts and favors to police officers vary from the free meals and police discounts given to patrol officers to exotic and expensive meals, expensive liquor, sports tickets, show tickets, television sets, refrigerators, free apartment rents, free use of vehicles, vacations, and the list goes on. These are given to ranking officers up the chain of command, including those with the power to award contracts or purchase orders such as deputy chiefs, chiefs, and commissioners. I will return to this issue later.

Police professional associations should address and issue statements addressing the free banquets, hospitality rooms, and "goodie bags" handed out by law enforcement suppliers and vendors at the meetings. Recall the old Mafia saw, "if you throw enough bread on the water some will come back."

Chapter 6

LAW ENFORCEMENT CODE OF ETHICS – PARAGRAPHS 4 AND 5

I RECOGNIZE the badge of my office as a symbol of public faith, and I accept it as a public trust to be held so long as I am true to the ethics of police service. I will never engage in acts of bribery, nor will I condone such acts by other police officers. I will cooperate with all legally authorized agencies and their representatives in the pursuit of justice.

While it may be true that all social relationships are based on trust, there is a special trust embodied in the law enforcement badge. We in our interactions with others trust them to behave in appropriate and accepted fashion. Society is based on this principle. We trust others to be honest, truthful, and respectful of our feelings in their dealings with us. We trust that others will treat us as persons and not objects. We trust that parents will take care of their children. We trust that people will pay their debts.

In some people, we place more trust than others. We trust that our husbands and wives will not violate their marriage vows. We trust that our children will obey our wishes. We trust our friends and relatives. We all know people who claim not to trust anyone and we in turn do not trust them. I put trust in quotes because we all know that not all persons act in appropriate and acceptable ways. That is why societies define some forms as deviant (or norm violating) behavior all the way from inappropriate social behavior (picking one's nose at the table, not observing standards of personal hygiene, overuse of certain words of profanity, talking in church, etc.) to crime. Societies have formal and informal means of social control to control and discipline those who do not act appropriately. We rely on social groups to enforce the informal means of social control. The criminal justice system exists to control and punish those who violate those behaviors considered serious enough to be enacted into law.

The law enforcement officer, as the most visible representative of the formal social control system and our representative of the democracy we live in, is given a special trust. He or she, after taking their oath of office, is given the badge as a symbol of that trust. Because of the authority we give them, we expect that they will always engage in lawful and ethical behavior. We also expect them to not condone unlawful and unethical behavior by other law enforcement officers. This special relationship we have with our law enforcement officers is what makes their unethical behavior so serious and disturbing. The professional law enforcement officer who adheres to the **Law Enforcement Code of Ethics** recognizes and understands this special relationship.

> **I KNOW** that I alone am responsible for my own standard of professional performance and will take every opportunity to enhance and improve my level of knowledge and competence.

This paragraph reinforces the principle that professional performance and adherence to the **Code** is a personal commitment. The devil or the peer group (other law enforcement officers) cannot be blamed for violations of the **Code**. The law enforcement officer will have to accept personal responsibility for his or her unethical behavior. They will have to accept personal responsibility for condoning the unethical behavior of others that they are aware of.

This paragraph of the **Code** also makes clear that professional development in the field of law enforcement is also a personal commitment. The professional law enforcement officer will take advantage of every opportunity to enhance his or her knowledge and competence in the field of law enforcement. The department also shares in this responsibility. They have the duty to provide a continuous process of training throughout the officer's career.

> **I WILL** constantly strive to achieve these objectives and ideals, dedicating myself before GOD to my chosen profession . . . LAW ENFORCEMENT.

Chapter 7

MAJOR LAW ENFORCEMENT ETHICAL VIOLATIONS

INTRODUCTION

In the first edition, the author divided the major ethical violations into police corruption and other forms of police misconduct. The distinction between the two categories was the presence or absence of a material reward or gain. After thirty years of researching the topic, discussions with numerous colleagues, and input from countless police officers in training sessions, I have come to the conclusion that the ethical violations can actually be better categorized as organizational/rule violations, corruption, and abuse of authority (Barker, 2002).

ORGANIZATIONAL/RULE VIOLATIONS

Technically speaking, all ethical violations involve a violation of an organizational rule or accepted police standard. However, corruption and abuse of authority will be discussed separately because they are serious breeches of established police standards, laws, and often constitutional guarantees. They are usually acted on external to the organization – **external reaction** – often in addition to some departmental action. In most cases, they cause some scandal for the department and draw a lot of media attention. The penalty for these acts (corruption and abuse of authority) can be either criminal or civil or both in some cases. For some acts of abuse of authority the agency and/or political entity may be held liable as well as the individual/s involved. Most, but not all (see "Sexual Misconduct" and "Police Lying") of the ethical violations included under the category of organizational/rule violations involve departmental discipline or termination – **internal reaction**. The most common organizational/rule violations that involve ethical issues are drinking on duty, use of drugs, police lying, accepting gratuities, and sexual misconduct. In recent years, the misuse of office computers and law enforcement databases has become an ethical problem and sometimes a means to commit acts of corruption.

Drinking on Duty

Obviously, drinking on duty is a serious ethical violation and contrary to organizational rules. The officer who drinks on the job presents a grave threat to citizens and his/her fellow officers. He or she is armed and usually in command of a powerful police vehicle. Mistakes made by an intoxicated police officer can cause death or serious injury to citizens and other police officers. A Fort Worth police officer resigned form the department and is currently awaiting trial for intoxication manslaughter after crashing his city vehicle and killing a female driver of another car (Boyd, 2010). The officer's alcohol level was twice the legal limit.

Drinking on duty, like similar organizational/rule violations such as sleeping on duty, may be a symptom of alienation from the job. It can also be the result of boredom, monotony, and opportunity combined with ineffectual supervision. Alcoholism among officers can be a serious problem because of the abundant opportunities they have to drink while on duty.

Use of Drugs

The use of drugs, other than alcohol on or off duty, by police officers has received a great deal of attention in recent years. Carter and Stephens (1991), in their seminal work on police drug use, arrived at two conclusions: (1) a strong impression that incidents of police corruption associated with either drug trafficking by law enforcement officers or through the assistance of police is increasing. This conclusion has certainly been supported by recent events (more on this later) and (2) some police officers use drugs as a recreational activity. The recreational use, although in most cases illegal, is generally handled internally as an organizational rule violation. We can also add to this that police officers with addiction problems have increased.

Police officers often come from a population group where the use of drugs, particularly marijuana, is prevalent and have been exposed to their use as recreation. In fact, and recognized by many agencies, some officers have been occasional and recreational drug users prior to joining the force. Some of these same officers might agree with the rationalizations offered for off-duty drug use, particularly if the drugs are in the "less dangerous" categories, i.e., not crack, cocaine, LSD, heroin, or methamphetamine.

The use/misuse of steroids and human growth hormones has become a problem in some police agencies. A Paw Paw, Michigan officer was terminated from the department and charged with possession of Fluoxymestrone, an anabolic steroid (Hall, 2010). His codefendant, the owner of three fitness centers, was charged with the delivery/manufacture of the steroid. Three Akron, Ohio police officers have been arrested on steroid-related charges in an investigation of anabolic steroid use in the department (Trexler, 2010). An officer must face the fact that such use is against the law, unethical, and forbidden by police rules and regulations. One must also acknowledge that even in those population groups where occasional drug use does take place, not all engage in this behavior. One must also face the troubling danger that recreational use leaves the officer subject to blackmail by his suppler or those using with him/her. Furthermore, recreational use can easily lead to instances of corruption, addiction and drug use on duty.

A veteran detective with the Schenectady, New York police department was allowed to retire and keep her pension before being convicted of official misconduct and criminal diversion of prescription medication (Nelson, 2010). She was addicted to prescription medicine.

Police Lying

The **Law Enforcement Code of Ethics** paragraph 4 stated that law enforcement officers should be "honest in thought and deed in both my personal and official life." That would imply that officers should never lie, a standard that is impossible to meet in police work. In fact, one can say that lying and other deceptive practices are an integral part of the police officer's working environment (Barker & Carter,

1994). Police officers lie to citizens, each other, suspects, victims, the media, in court, and to other criminal justice officials. These lies and deceptive practices vary as to whether or not they should be considered as ethical violations – organizational rule violations, a means to commit corruption, abuse of authority – or are necessary for the police to accomplish their tasks. For that reason, we will discuss the patterns of police lying here and again in the sections on corruption and abuse of authority.

Accepted Lying

Lies in this category are those considered to be an accepted part of an officer's working environment. The lies are told because they fulfill a defined law enforcement mission. The police organization and its members will freely admit that they are engaging in deceptive practices. The most obvious example of accepted lying is the lies and deceptive practices engaged in by undercover officers. Secret and consensual crime operations could probably not be carried out without some deceptive practices. Police officers engaged in these activities must not only conceal their identity, but they must talk, act, and dress out of character. They must fabricate all kinds of stories to perform these duties. One can hardly imagine that FBI Special Agent Joseph Pistone could have operated for six years in the Mafia without the numerous lies he had to tell (Pistone, 1987). He was so successful that he was asked to become a "made" member of the Mafia before he was withdrawn. In a more recent case, ATF Special Agent Billy Queen spent two years with the extremely violent *Mongols Motorcycle Club* (Queen, 2005). He had to lie every day to keep from being killed. Special Agent Queen also became his chapter's secretary treasurer, a position that allowed for the successful prosecution of several members of this Outlaw Motorcycle Gang. More recently, ATF special agent Jay Dobyns spent two years undercover with the notorious *Hells Angels Motorcycle Club* (Dobyns & Johnson-Shelton, 2009).

The overwhelming majority of undercover operations are neither as fascinating nor as dangerous as working with the Mafia or Outlaw Motorcycle Gangs or some other organized crime group. The most common operations occur in routine vice operations dealing with prostitution, gambling, or narcotics. However, this area is not without its problems. Marx (1985) pointed out that sometimes these practices could lead to a situation in which the police go beyond determining if a suspect is breaking the law and attempt to see if the person can be induced into breaking the law. This sort of activity raises the specter of entrapment. The author, although not a fan of the popular TV show *Cops*, has seen several episodes where one could argue that this indeed happened. The "Dirty Harry" problem, where some officers believe that the end justifies the means, raises the question as to what extent supposedly "good police practices" warrant or justify ethically, politically, or legally suspect means to achieve law enforcement activities (Klockers, 1980).

Encouraging the commission of a crime may be a legally accepted police practice when the offender acts as a willing victim or the officer's actions facilitate the commission of a crime which was going to be committed in the first place. However, it is possible for "encouragement" to lead the suspect to raise the defense of entrapment. According to *Black's Law Dictionary*, entrapment is "the act of officers or agents of the government inducing a person to commit a crime not contemplated by him, for the purpose of instituting a criminal prosecution against him" (277). In order for the defense of entrapment to prevail, the defendant must show that the officer or his/her agent (informant in most cases) has gone beyond providing the encouragement and opportunity for the commission of a crime and through trickery, fraud, or other deception has induced the suspect to commit a crime. This defense is raised far more times than it is successful because the most often used legal criterion to determine entrapment is what is known as the "subjective test."

In the subjective test, the predisposition of the offender, rather than the objective methods of the law enforcement officers, is the key to determining entrapment (Skolnick, 1982; Marx, 1985; Stitt & James, 1985). This test makes it extremely difficult for a defendant with a criminal record to claim that he/she would not have committed the crime except for the action of the officer. Another test – the "objective test" – raised by a minority of the Supreme Court, has focused on the nature of the law enforcement officer's conduct rather than the predisposition of the offender (Stitt & James, 1985). For example, the objective test probably would examine whether the production of crack cocaine by a police organization for use in undercover drug arrests is proper and legal. In 1989, according to an *Associated Press* story, the Broward County Florida Sheriff's Department, not having enough crack to supply undercover officers, manufactured its own. The sheriff's department chemist made at least $20,000 worth of the illegal substance. Local defense attorneys raised the issue of entrapment. One public defender stated: "I think there's something sick about this whole system where the police make the product, sell the product and arrest people for buying the product" (*Birmingham Post Herald*, April 19, 1989: B 2).

What do you think? In my opinion, deceptive practices aside, having a law enforcement agent make an illegal drug and then sell it to others and then arrest those who buy it does raise a number of ethical and legal issues. The issue could arise today if an agent (informant) of the police manufactures methamphetamines with police knowledge and sells some or all of it to others under the officer's direction and the officer then arrests those who buy it. At what point do we draw the line to make a police undercover operation convincing? Fortunately, the manufacture of crack by the Broward County Sheriff's Department was stopped as soon as the media got wind of it. The current "war on drugs" raises similar issues in this area. Black-clad "Ninja Police" have been accused of violating citizens' civil rights as they stage "whoops raids" (wrong persons or wrong addresses), use unreliable and nonexistent informers and overly destructive search techniques in the war. There have been several successful civil suits that have awarded damages to complainants for police overzealousness in this area. The police must be careful that the ends do not become more important than the means of accomplishing them (more on this later). "Dirty Harry" and Andy Sipowitz may be characters we applaud on the screen or the TV, but we shouldn't want him working for our police department.

In addition to the accepted practices of lying, required for undercover operations, members of the police community often believe that it is proper to lie to the media or the public when it is necessary to protect the innocent, protect the image of the department, or calm the public in a crisis situation. The department's official policy may be one of openness and candor when dealing with the media. However, as a practical matter, members of the department may deny the existence of an investigation or "plant" erroneous information, i.e., disinformation, to protect an ongoing investigation. The untimely revelation of facts may alert the suspects and drive them underground or cause them to cease their illegal acts – often not a bad thing. Nevertheless, one could argue that public exposure of certain criminal activities – operation of serial rapists or killer – or the possibility of them might decrease the risk of injury or death.

Tolerated Lying

Tolerated lies are those recognized as lies by the police organization but tolerated as "necessary evils." They are situational or "white lies" told when it is not possible to explain the truth. For example, police officials will often claim to practice full enforcement of the laws at all times rather than try to explain the thorny issue of police discretionary decision making. At the scene of a crime, an officer may lie to a victim rather than admit that there is no chance to catch the perpetrator or recover stolen property. When asked by a relative if the victim suffered before dying, we would hope that the officer would be compassionate in his or her answer.

As one can imagine, the interrogation stage of an arrest is an area filled with examples of tolerated lying. According to many police officers and textbooks on the subject, telling the suspect that there is evidence to link him/her to the crime or that fellow suspects have confessed are "good" interrogation techniques. One could say that the ends justify the means. However, lies told under these circumstances could and have led innocent persons to succumb to the powerful persuasion of a police officer and admit to crimes they did not commit.

Deviant Lying

The third form of police lying has two forms: (1) **Deviant Lies in Support of Perceived Legitimate Goals** and (2) **Deviant Lies in Support of Illegitimate Goals**.

The first, lies told for perceived legitimate goals, usually occur to put criminals in jail, prevent crime, and perform other policing responsibilities. They will be discussed in depth in the category Abuse of Authority, as they are a means to affect Noble Cause Injustice.

Deviant lies in support of illegitimate goals are told to affect an act of corruption or to protect an officer from organizational discipline or civil and/or criminal liability. The officer who commits perjury in court may do so to "fix" a criminal prosecution for monetary reward. In fact, lying and/or perjury in court or before other criminal justice officials are an absolute necessity in departments where corrupt acts occur on a routine basis. Sooner or later, every police officer who engages in corrupt acts or observes fellow officers engaging in corrupt acts will face the possibility of having to lie under oath to protect himself/herself or fellow officers. Several years ago, an Orange County, California sheriff was sentenced to five years in prison after he was secretly recorded attempting to convince an assistant sheriff to lie to a federal grand jury to cover up the sheriff's bribe taking.

There is always the distinct possibility that engaging in other forms of organizational rule violations will lead to deviant lying. To avoid the possibility of discipline and in some cases criminal and/or civil liability, the officer who engages in a rule violation may have to lie on an official report, to his/her supervisor, and possibly during testimony. For example, the officer who engages in a police action (pursuit, use of force, etc.) that is against the law or the department's policies, procedures, or rules and the action results in death or serious injury may have to lie or commit perjury to protect himself/herself or fellow officers. In 2008, one New Orleans police officer was fired and a second was suspended for 80 days when 5 officers lied to investigators and one coerced a civilian to file a false police report to cover-up a fight between off-duty NOPD officers and a city transit worker. Four Hollywood, Florida officers and a sergeant were suspended when they were recorded on a dash cam fabricating a story to frame a driver for a traffic accident. A police officer had rear-ended the victim and the police were trying to make it the victim's fault.

Probably the most egregious example of police lying to avoid criminal and civil liability in American history occurred on the Danziger Bridge in New Orleans in the aftermath of Hurricane Katrina on September 4, 2005. The story is unfolding at this time but the facts as they appear now are as follows (DOJ, February 24, 2010; DOJ, March 30, 2010; DOJ, April 16, 2010). Five members of one family were walking across the Danziger Bridge to get food and supplies when they were encountered by seven New Orleans Police Department (NOPD) officers. The officers in a rental truck were responding to a call for police assistance. The officers, without provocation or justification, opened fire killing one person and injuring four. The officers then went to the other side of the bridge and encountered two brothers going to a dentist's office. The officers opened fire on the brothers, killing one, a severely disabled man.

Thus far four NOPD officers have pleaded guilty to federal charges involved in the cover-up of the police involved shootings. A fifth officer has pleaded guilty to writing a false charging document and lying to investigators and a grand jury. The first to plead guilty was a supervising lieutenant who admitted that he participated in the cover-up by writing false reports about the incident, planting a gun and witness statements. The lieutenant admitted that when he arrived on the scene, he noticed that there were no guns on or near the victims and no other evidence to support the officers' story of the shooting. He said he knew it was a "bad shoot." That is when he participated in the cover-up. Another officer who pleaded guilty to the cover-up said that he saw a supervisor repeatedly kick or stomp on the second victim as he lay wounded and dying. The Danziger Bridge shootings are one of several shooting incidents that occurred post Katrina and are under investigation by federal authorities. There is no way of knowing what affect, if any, these and other investigations will have on the New Orleans Police Department, but it is obvious that the department needs structural and cultural change.

Accepting Gratuities

One can argue that accepting gratuities – free coffee, drinks, meals, liquor, services, free admission to entertainment, etc. – should be included in corruption – as I did for years and in the first edition of this book – or considered as a nonthreatening fringe benefit as Kania (1988) does. One could also view accepting gratuities as an ethicist would define immoral acts: "immoral acts negatively affect the welfare of the person who commits the acts, either because they diminish moral character or because they form a 'slippery slope' that leads to even worse actions" (Welfel, 1997: 135). Furthermore, if any services (more protection, faster response, etc.) are provided in return, it "takes time and unjustly deprives other members of the public of the attention they deserve" (Delattre, 1989: 10).

Kania (1988) argues that accepting gratuities does not lead officers into corrupt acts. This view is shared by numerous police officers and has been expressed over and over again in the training sessions I have conducted. There seems to be the idea among many law enforcement officers that there is some kind of "divine right" for the police when it comes to accepting gratuities, especially drinks – not alcoholic – and meals. Some officers go further and demand their entitled "freebies." Those who feel that accepting gratuities does not lead to any other violations may be right for most officers. However, many officers have been "sucked" into the corruption habit through freebies. What became known as the Dowd Test after New York City Police Officer Michael Dowd (convicted of drug trafficking), involved getting officers to accept small gratuities and then move them into more serious acts. Kania says that the Dowd Test was successful "because the rules [departmental] define otherwise normally motivated behavior as corrupt. It is normal to accept *minor* gifts from people who wish to maintain good social relations with us" (Kania, 1988: 37, italics added). Sounds like members of Congress justifying accepting gratuities from lobbyists. Kania ignores that many of those "normal" people wishing to maintain good relations with police officers have a great deal to gain by good relations with cops. Kania also fails to realize that accepting gratuities goes up the chain of command to officials who make purchasing decisions and influence other government officials.

It is also true that some of these offers come from "respectable citizens" who may be "freely" giving minor gifts to their police officers. Some may not expect anything in return when the gift is offered. However, at a later time such respectable citizens or one of their employees, relatives, or friends may get a ticket, be arrested for a "non-serious" misdemeanor, need help with a licensing agency, or want a record check on a prospective employee, son-in-law, or the "dirt bag" going out with his daughter. Who are they going to call for help? The officers who have been accepting their minor gifts are now in a difficult situation. They can wax indignantly, saying there is nothing they can do (which is probably true), promise to try to help in order to "cool" them out, or they may actually find a way to help their benefactor, even though they may have to bend a rule to do so. Article 9 of the **Canons of Police Ethics** specifically addresses this issue.

> **Article 9. Gifts and Favors.** The law enforcement officer, representing government bears the heavy responsibility of maintaining, in his own conduct, the honor and integrity of all government institutions. He shall, therefore, guard against placing himself in a position where any person can expect special consideration or in which the public can reasonably assume that special consideration is being given. *Thus, he should be firm in refusing gifts, favors, or gratuities, large or small, which can in the*

public mind be interpreted as capable of influencing his judgment in the discharge of his duties. (IACP, 1981. italics added.)

Michael Josephenson of the Josephenson Institute for Ethics (http://web2.airmail.net/slf/spring94/dowd.html) poses two questions for officers concerning gratuities: (1) why take it? And (2) if you were not a police officer, would that person still be offering you that freebie? Furthermore, one must consider the impropriety of uniformed police officers accepting free and discounted meals and other services. Citizens observing this behavior do not join in philosophical debates on this issue. To them, the officers are freeloaders. At least that is what numerous citizens have told this author.

At times, citizens observe police officers demanding gratuities from reluctant businesses. A Daytona, Florida police lieutenant was fired in 2008 after complaints from a local *Starbucks*. The lieutenant would visit the store six times a day and cut in front of irate customers while registering his demands. The lieutenant was rehired after an arbitrator ruled he should not have been fired. The lieutenant is now under investigation for illegally parking his unmarked patrol car in a handicapped parking spot while he refereed a basketball tournament (AP a, 2010). Police executives and city officials often complain about the interference of arbitrators in efforts to discipline officers. The mayor of Pittsburg recently urged "public safety personnel to clean up their act" after a rash of off-duty incidents by police and firefighters. He is quoted as saying "We've disciplined officers. We've disciplined firefighters. . . . We've fired them, terminated them. Only to find that they've won their jobs back" in arbitration (Lord, R, 2010).

One also wonders how, and who, will define minor gifts. Is a cup of coffee at $1.00 a cup a minor gift, what is a minor meal, one under $5.00 at a fast food restaurant or one under $50.00 at an upscale restaurant? Should there be a sliding scale based on rank and assignment? Certain places are known as police hangouts; therefore, should the definition take into account only minor gifts to the beat officer or all officers? Does it become more than minor when there is more than one officer? The questions could go on ad nauseam.

The confusing nature of making distinctions about the value and nature of these minor gifts was made clear to me over 20 years ago. In 1983, the State of Alabama's Ethics Commission issued an advisory opinion on free meals given to police officers. Part of that opinion follows:

Any law enforcement agent or officer coming under the Ethics law who accepts a free meal or discounted meal with the understanding that he will devote more of his time to insuring protection for the restaurant or eating establishment to a greater degree than another restaurant which does not offer free or discounted meals violates Section 36–25–6 of the Alabama Ethics law . . .

At the time the advisory opinion was rendered, the argument was raised among some law enforcement groups that free meals or cut-rate meals were only unethical if there was an understanding that the officer would devote more time to protecting these eating establishments over those who do not. Therefore, the conclusion was no understanding or intention on the part of the officers to do this, then no ethical violation. Several years later an incident occurred which proved explicitly what I had maintained was always implied in such arrangements.

An irate citizen complained to the city council of one of the municipalities about city police officers receiving free and discounted meals from one of the fast food chains. Her complaint named a particular restaurant and its location. The complaint received wide media coverage. A police captain, identified by name in the newspaper, was quoted as saying, "you could not buy a police officer from his department with a free hamburger." According to the newspaper, he went on to say that the woman who complained was a troublemaker and there was nothing wrong with officers receiving free or discounted meals.

The last comment caused me to write a letter to the editor. In the letter, which was published, I stated that there was something wrong with police officers accepting free or discounted meals. I pointed out that the **Law Enforcement Code of Ethics**, as well as the captain's own department, prohibited such behavior. I raised other ethical issues in my letter and suggested that if law enforcement officers could not live by the **Code**, then it should be changed. I pointed out that his department had a rule against accepting *any* gratuities. I pointed out that should be changed also if he or his department thought there was nothing wrong with accepting free or discounted meals. I also stated that there were numerous professional police officers who did not agree with this captain. The matter was closed, I thought.

Several weeks after my letter was printed, this very same fast food restaurant and a number of customers were robbed by a group of "gang bangers" from a nearby metropolitan area. An unnamed police captain was quoted in the media as saying, "If they hadn't stopped the free meals, there would probably have been a cop in there when it happened." In my opinion, that statement is pure and simple extortion. No free meals, no protection.

Other officers in other cities have sanctioned businesses and others who have refused to give the perks of the job. They have excluded businesses from routine security checks, customers have been harassed, and citations have been issued for obscure and seldom enforced violations.

The Alabama Ethics Commission in the same advisory opinion cited above made another statement that I wholeheartedly agree with:

> . . . The Commission would find no unethical implications if **all** public employees were given discounts on meals in order to increase business by establishments, but to single out only those individuals who happen to carry a badge is difficult to understand even when done under the guise of tradition (Alabama Ethics Commission, July 6, 1983).

This was the same feeling that was held by the founders of the modern day police and a morally dangerous occupation. All gifts to the 1829 London Metropolitan Police had to be reported and approved (Reynolds, 1998: 153). However, gratuities, still forbidden, are also common among the British police, where some shops are known to be "GTP" (good to the police) (Holdaway, 1984: 43).

As stated earlier, discussing gratuities as if they were only minor gifts and favors given to patrol officers diverts attention from an even larger problem with this dangerous practice. Gifts and favors to police officers vary from the free meals and discounts given to patrol officers to the exotic and expensive meals, expensive liquor, sports tickets, show tickets, television sets, refrigerators, free apartment rents, free use of vehicles, vacations, and the list goes on given to ranking officers up the chain of command, including those with the power to award contracts or purchase orders, such as captains, deputy chiefs, chiefs, and commissioners. Former New York City Police Commissioner Bernard Kerik (2000–2001) is now inmate 84888-054 in a Maryland Prison after pleading guilty to two counts of tax fraud, one count of making a false statement on a loan application, and five counts of making false statements to the federal government while being vetted for the Secretary of Homeland Security position (Dolnick, 2009; James, 2009; Moritz, 2010). Kerik admitted that a New Jersey construction firm paid $165,000 for the renovations to his Bronx apartment and that he had contacted officials on their behalf. The $165K gratuity was certainly not minor and in all probability not the only one the disgraced former commissioner ever accepted.

The former Miami Chief of Police John Timoney had a formal complaint filed with the State Ethics Commission against him for violating Florida law governing acceptance of gifts by public officials (Anon p, 2007). The complaint involved a year's free use of an SUV from a local car dealership. The chief denied doing anything wrong but said that his use of the vehicle raised ethical question and asked for the city manager and the city's ethics board to determine if he did anything wrong. The Miami Police Department rules specifies that officers "shall not accept gifts, fees, goods or services" and the Florida law states that all gifts of a value over $100 must be reported. The chief claimed that it was not a gift but an "open-ended test drive." The chief purchased the SUV after the complaint was filed. The Miami-Dade Ethics Commission found that there was probable cause to believe that the law had been broken (Nielson, 2007). The Miami Civilian Investigative Panel ruled that the chief had violated multiple department rules. After almost a year of tumultuous rhetoric by the chief and other officials, including a no-confidence vote by the Fraternal Order of Police, the state and county ethics boards fined the chief $500 for failing to disclose the use of the SUV for over a year. The city manager also docked the chief a week's pay (Ovalle, 2009). It appears that this whole controversy could have been avoided if the chief had avoided a situation where even he admitted there was a perception of unethical behavior. One is left to wonder how the chief would have handled the matter if one of his subordinates had engaged in the same behavior, including disregarding subpoenas issued by the Miami Civilian Investigative Panel, as he did. Subordinates look to the behavior of those above them for clues to their own ethical behavior.

An unfolding case of the dangers of the acceptance of gratuities by police officers whatever rank has come to light with the recent conviction and sentencing of Fort Lauderdale, Florida lawyer Scott Rothstein (DOJ, 2010). Rothstein was sentenced to 50 years for operating a $1.2 billion Ponzi scheme through his law firm. For a Ponzi scheme to be successful the actors have to appear to be legitimate. What better way to appear legitimate than to surround yourself with police officials and officers? A fact recognized by Rothstein and his colleagues. Count 36 of the Indictment *USA v Scott Rothstein* states:

36. Defendant ROTHSTEIN and other co-conspirators utilized funds illegally obtained through the Ponzi scheme to hire members of local police departments to purportedly provide security of RRA and defendant ROTHSTEIN'S personal residence. Ponzi scheme funds were also used to provide **gratuities to high ranking members of police agencies in order to curry favor with police personnel and to deflect law enforcement scrutiny of the activities of RRA and defendant ROTHSTEIN** (Emphasis Added).

Broward County Sheriff's Office Lt. David Benjamin and Fort Lauderdale Police Chief Frank Adderley are cited in one newspaper article as recipients of gifts and meals from Rothstein (Sherman, Weaver, & Lebovich, 2009). Allegedly Lt. Benjamin, Broward County Sheriff's Office executive officer, before being removed when the scandal broke, started his own consulting business with $30,000 in funding from Rothstein, and was a guest in Rothstein's luxury box at a professional football game. Lt. Benjamin escorted Rothstein to a Gulfstream jet when he fled the country to Morocco when the scheme blew up. Fort Lauderdale Chief of Police Adderley has admitted to taking a jet flight with Rothstein to New York to see New York Jets-Miami Dolphin game (Wallman, 2010). According to newspaper accounts, at least 28 high-ranking police officers detectives, undercover officers, and the department's spokesperson worked for Rothstein, earning $40 to $50 an hour (Wallman, 2010). The two officers who coordinated the Rothstein work have been suspended. This is not the first example of criminal enterprises freely distributing gratuities to police personnel. The Mafia and other organized crime groups have done this for decades.

Gratuities, no matter the value, should not be allowed in police work, they cause too much trouble and embarrassment. Delattre (1989) states that the prevailing view, myself included, is that all police gratuities should be prohibited. There is always the danger of creating an environment of tolerance. The IACP's Model Policy: Standards of Conduct (Section 8: Abuse of Law Enforcement Powers or Position) states:

a. Officers shall report any unsolicited gifts, gratuities, or other items of value that they are offered and shall provide a full report of the circumstances of their receipt (IACP, 1997).

Such mandatory reporting practices would make public the offering and accepting of gratuities and provide a check on any abuse of power or position by police officers. It would have a chilling effect on any person, business, or group who had an ulterior motive in the offer. Now, we will turn to more serious organizational/rule violations that involve no debate.

Sexual Misconduct

Police sexual misconduct while on duty has occurred ever since the creation of the London Metropolitan Police and before them in the Watch and Ward systems. Obviously, male officers come into contact with females during their routine police duties. These contacts often occur under conditions that provide opportunities for illicit sex. The women and the officers are frequently alone and supervision of the officers on patrol is often minimal. Officers working the late night shifts have the added cover of darkness and little traffic on the road. The officer also has the opportunity to stop women coming from a night of drinking. An intoxicated woman may decide that her sexual favors are a small price to pay in order to avoid an arrest for driving while intoxicated. Utah's Peace Officers Standard and Training Council (POST) reports that sexual misconduct offenses are the most common reason for officers to lose their certification or be suspended (Anon h. 2006). Among the offenses reported to the *Utah Post* are rape, attempted sodomy, child sexual abuse, and having sex with inmates, parolees, or people on probation. Sexual misconduct offenses are more common than excessive force, falsifying reports, or driving under the influence. Allan Sapp (1994) identified seven categories of sexually motivated or sexual harassment behaviors by police officers that are directly related to occupational duties. We begin our discussion with his categories.

Sapp's Categories of Police Sexual Misconduct

NONSEXUAL CONTACT. This category involves behaviors that are usually sexually motivated without direct sexual actions or inferences. The female citizen may not be aware of the underlying motivations of the officer. However, Sapp says that this behavior is a form of sexual harassment because the officer initiates the contact without legal basis or probable cause. The officer is motivated by a desire to get a closer look at the female or gain information about her. The invalid traffic stop is a good example of this category.

Officers may also stop a female on foot under one pretense or another to obtain information or initiate a conversation. Some of these stops may be followed up by more direct sexual contacts. For example, in 2008, a Scranton, Pennsylvania police officer initiated several traffic stops with the same woman and then went to her place of employment on another occasion and in uniform exposed his penis to her and said "You know there are feelings between us" (McDonald, May 12, 2010). The officer pleaded guilty to charges of official oppression and indecent assault and the city paid $145,000 to settle the civil suit. Curiously, the then Department of Public Safety defended the city by saying that there was nothing but the officer's drug problem to indicate possible misconduct.

VOYEURISTIC CONTACTS. Some officers spend their time seeking opportunities to view unsuspecting women partially clad or nude. They are literally "Peeping Toms" in uniform. The most common form of this category is officers who seek out parked cars in lover's lanes hoping to observe sexual acts. They sometimes park their cars and sneak up on the occupants.

CONTACTS WITH CRIME VICTIMS. Sapp says that female victims of crime are particularly susceptible to sexual harassment by police officers. They are vulnerable because they are often emotionally upset and turn to the police for support and assistance. Unnecessary callbacks to the residence of the female are one of the most common forms of this behavior. The officer's frequent trips to female victim's residence are for the purpose of initiating some sexual contact.

Sex crimes victims are also susceptible to sexual harassment by police officers. Some of this is unintentional when it results from a lack of sensitivity and knowledge on the officer's part. However, when an officer questions the victims beyond the depth of details needed for investigations purposes, this is sexual harassment.

CONTACTS WITH OFFENDERS. This may be the most prevalent form of police sexual misconduct. Offenders, both male and female, are in a vulnerable position when it comes to being a victim of sexual harassment or sexual contact. Offenders are aware of the authority of the officer and that, if they have committed an offense, particularly alcohol or drug intoxication, their complaints may be disregarded or played down. Offenders are subject to sexual demands or body searches, frisks or pat downs that lead to fondling.

Vulnerability increases when that person is in a correctional setting or is an undocumented alien. Custer County, Oklahoma Sheriff Mike Burgess was sentenced to 79 years in prison for sexually abusing female inmates and drug court defendants (AP g. 3, 24, 2009). In effect, the sheriff ran a sex-slave operation from jail. A drug court defendant said that the sheriff forced her to have sex with him or he would send her to prison. The former sheriff was convicted of five counts of second degree rape, three counts of bribery, two counts of forcible sodomy, kidnapping, sexual battery for groping a female deputy, and engaging in a pattern of criminal offenses. A former Anaheim, California officer pleaded guilty to sexually assaulting three women, one who did not have legal papers and was threatened with deportation (AP e, 5/17'2010). The officer forced her to perform oral sex on him. A Broward County, Florida sheriff's deputy is currently awaiting trial for five counts of sexual battery in a position of control or authority, four counts of armed false imprisonment, four counts of battery and one count of stalking or preying on illegal residents (BSO Release August 3, 2009). The deputy, a seven-year veteran and 2008 Employee of the Year, is openly gay and is charged with sexually assaulting eight undocumented Latino migrants ranging in age from 17–30. The former officer is being held in protective custody without bail until his trial.

Sexual misconduct with offenders occurs in all types of settings and police agencies. A 13-year veteran NYPD detective is charged with violating the civil rights of three women whom he forced to have sex with him while working as a narcotics detective (Anon d. May 16, 2010). According to the criminal information, it is alleged that he told one women she would go to jail and lose her children unless she had sex with him. A 10-year veteran FBI special agent pleaded guilty to wire fraud charges related to improper sexual relationships with the wife of a man he investigated in two separate charges (AP f. 3, 23, 2009). In the plea agreement the former special agent admitted engaging in an improper intimate relationship in violation of federal law and FBI regulations.

Two New Jersey Transit police officers who were accused of raping an intoxicated women who asked for their help were convicted of official misconduct and sentenced to three years in prison in 2007 (Conte, 2010). She asked the officers to help her find her car. After finding her car the victim said she would sleep it off in her car. The officers convinced her to instead drive to an isolated location where they raped her. A civil jury awarded the victim $760,000.

Drunk-driving suspects are frequent victims of this form of sexual misconduct. A Des Moines, Iowa police officer was convicted of trying to attack a suspected drunk-driving woman in his squad car. The woman allegedly said that she would do anything just to go home (Anon j, 2010). The officer drove to an isolated location and climbed in the back seat and groped the woman. The woman called and complained. The officer had only been a police officer for 18 months and had already been suspended for two days after making an inappropriate comment to a woman (Finney, 2010). A history of complaints and disciplinary actions is often present in officers who are accused, arrested, indicted, and convicted of sexual misconduct and other ethical violations.

CONTACTS WITH JUVENILES – OFFENDERS AND OTHERS [original modified]. On occasion, police officers have sexually harassed or had sexual contacts with runaways, truants, and delinquents and other vulnerable juveniles. In 2009, a Jackson County, Missouri deputy sheriff was sentenced to 14 years after pleading guilty to sexually assaulting a 15-year-old girl in his police car. The deputy found the victim and her friends in a park drinking. He told the others to leave and forced the teenager to perform oral sex on him. A 16-year veteran, Atlanta, Georgia police officer has been charged with sexual battery, enticing a child of indecent purposes, violation of oath of office, exploitation of a minor, and child molestation for allegedly molesting a 13-year-old he met when responding to a domestic violence call (AP h., 2010). The officer is alleged to have asked the girl to send nude pictures to him and to have groped her during visits to her home. The victim reported his behavior to the school resource officer. A Pennsylvania state trooper was sentenced to five to 10 years for assaulting at least four women he stopped; one was a 14-year-old runaway.

Police officers have had improper sexual contacts with juveniles or teenagers that they encountered while performing their special assignments, such as school resource officers or when the victims were ride-a-longs. In 2008, two Tarpon Springs, Florida police officers were under investigation for "possible improper conduct with juveniles (Anon c November 12, 2008). One of the officers met the subject of his attention, a 17-year-old high school student, while he worked as a school resource officer. The other officer met his victim through the department's ride-a-long program. This officer was fired following a complaint from his wife. A New York City sanitation police officer who also served as an instructor and public affairs officer for Staten Island's division of the national Navy Sea Cadets program was sentenced to eight years in prison for sexually molesting two teenage girls in the program (Donnelly, 2010). He would molest the girls in their restricted barracks during weekend Cadets outings.

SEXUAL SHAKEDOWNS. In this category, police officers demand sexual services from prostitutes or other citizens involved in illegal or illicit activities. A Houston officer was arrested on four counts of sexual assault after a police sting caught him in the act of taking a police decoy to a secluded location and patting her down (Dulai, 2010). It appears that his four victims were prostitutes whom he stopped and took to secluded locations and forced them to undress and engage in sex. After numerous complaints, the department put a female officer on the street and watched him stop her, take her to a secluded location, and pat her down. He was immediately arrested.

A Tennessee state trooper was indicted for taping sex acts with a porn star after disregarding illegal painkillers found in her car after a traffic stop. Two Philadelphia, Pennsylvania police officers were convicted of forcing a stripper who was getting off work to have sex with them on numerous occasions. A Greece, New York police officer was sentenced to two to six years for coercing a woman he stopped to have sex with him. Women who have agreed to act as confidential informants are vulnerable to sexual extortion. A confidential informant for the West Central Illinois Task Force claims that a deputy assigned to the task force forced her to have sex in his car and home. She also alleges that the deputy pressured her to set up a drug buy with a man who was not dealing drugs. The deputy resigned after the allegations were made. A Clinton, South Carolina officer was sentenced to six months after pleading guilty to misconduct in office after forcing a drug suspect to perform oral sex on him for not being charged for drug possession. He was fired from Clinton and hired by another department when the charges were filed (Anon e, 2010). The problem of "gypsy cops," cops fired from one agency or resigning under suspicious circumstances and then being hired by another agency will be discussed later. These are sexual activities involving an unwilling victim who yields solely on the basis of the police authority to arrest and prosecute. Rape is the correct term for this behavior.

CITIZEN-INITIATED SEXUAL CONTACTS. The female citizen and not the officer initiate some sexual contacts. Most police departments have stories about "police groupies" who are attracted to uniforms, weapons, or the authority of the police. Police officers also get calls from lonely or mentally disturbed women who want attention or affection. On occasion, women will commit minor traffic violations as a ruse to see if the officer is interested in sexual contact. Women also seek sexual contact in return for favors, preferential treatment, or additional protection. Obviously, women working in certain illegal occupations such as prostitution or pornography have a great deal to gain from a good working relationship with the police.

Many of the behaviors Sapp cited involve criminal violations. Those identified by Kraska and Kappeler (1995) in their study are definitely crimes. They identified 124 cases of police sexual violations; 37 of the cases were sexual assaults and rapes committed by on-duty police officers against female citizens.

Sexual Predators

Sadly, in addition to the categories identified by Sapp, there are other examples of police sexual misconduct. One of the most disturbing is **sexual predators** who commit their deviant activities in an occupation that provides ample opportunities. The former Chief of Police of Minneapolis Park, Minnesota is charged with multiple counts of child sexual abuse that took place during the 14 years he was chief and when he was a science teacher before becoming chief. The gay Broward County deputy who was preying on undocumented immigrants, mentioned earlier, would be classified as a sexual predator. A 10-year NYPD veteran was convicted of the sexual abuse of two women he met through his duties as a community affairs officer (Eligon, 2010). He was also convicted in a separate case of coercing a woman to give him oral sex to rip up a summons. A pending case involves a rape of another woman.

One wonders if the job attracts sexual deviants or if inadequate background checks are responsible for them coming on the job. Given the large number of sexual misconduct offenses identified by researchers, newspapers, and police misconduct websites, it is probably a combination of the two. The occupation with its numerous opportunities for sexual encounters – consensual and coerced – uneven power relations between the citizens and officers, and the code of silence for infractions by officers may attract sexual deviants and less than thorough background checks may fail to screen them out.

Sexual Harassment in the Workplace

There have been allegations and documented cases of sexual harassment in the workplace every since women joined police organizations. There have also been instances of male officers sexually harassing other male officers. A Los Angeles judge awarded $350,000 to a sheriff's deputy who claimed that his supervisor harassed him (Anon, m, 2010; Hetherman, 2010). The sordid details of the allegations include the supervisor asking if he ever engaged in oral sex with a man and telling him to bend over for a rectal examination. The victim also alleged that the supervisor slipped his finger in his underwear touching his rear end in the department locker room. The supervisor resigned under pressure before the lawsuit went to trial.

Misuse of Computers and Law Enforcement Databases

At least weekly there are reports of employees in all work settings misusing their office computers and company databases. The law enforcement occupation is not safe from these worker transgressions. Police departments have access to national databases such as the National Crime Information Center (NCIC) and the National Law Enforcement Telecommunication System (NLETS) as well as state systems such as state motor vehicle records, criminal warrant checks, and wanted information. Access to these databases can be used for corrupt purposes. A San Diego police officer pleaded guilty to running criminal record checks for drug traffickers (DOJ, 2009). A Harris County, Texas sheriff's deputy was indicted for disclosing confidential information from the department's National Crime Information Center (NCIC) for cash (DOJ, 2010). A U.S. Customs Agent (now Immigration and Customs Enforcement) was found guilty of accessing the Treasury Enforcement Communication System (TECS) open to federal agents and providing access to NCIC and TECS and selling the information (McCullagh, 2008). Examples of this misconduct occur in other countries. In 2007, a London Metropolitan police officer was charged with using the police computer database to blackmail people (Anon 1, 2007). The constable would threaten to reveal incriminating information unless they paid him.

Law enforcement officers have accessed computers and databases for personal reasons – viewing pornography, running background checks, etc. In May 2010, three Northumberland County, Virginia sheriff's deputies were fired for viewing pornography websites on officer computers (Moore, 2010). Law enforcement officers have used police databases to check up on daughters' boyfriends and suitors of her family members.

Chapter 8

POLICE CORRUPTION

INTRODUCTION

Police corruption is defined as any proscribed act involving the misuse of the officer's official position for money or money's worth. Other than for a few minor word changes this is the same definition developed by Julian Roebuck and I over 30 years ago (Barker & Roebuck, 1973). Three elements identify police corruption: (1) the behavior must be forbidden by law, rule, regulation, ethical standard. (2) The behavior must involve the misuse of the officer's official position, i.e., the officer must do something that he or she should not do, or fail to do something that he or she should do. Corrupt acts can occur off duty if that act is somehow related to the officer's employment as a sworn police officer. For example, the officer could learn of confidential information related to an individual and convey this information for money to that individual or another while off duty. The officer could also, during his or her normal patrol duties, "case" businesses for robberies or burglaries. (3) The reward – third element – for corrupt acts must be money or money's worth. It should be pointed out that the definition applies to corrupt police behavior by law enforcement officers at all levels of government – local, county, state, special district, and federal. I previously identified the following types of police corruption.

Barker's Typology of Police Corruption

KICKBACKS. This refers to money, goods and services accepted from such "legitimate" businesses and individuals such as towing companies, ambulances, garages, lawyers, doctors, undertakers, taxi cabs, service stations, moving companies, etc.

All of the businesses or individuals cited above have something to gain from a good working relationship with their local police. Many of the business people listed above freely distribute their cards to police officers and indicate their willingness to "take care of the officer" if they receive referrals from the officer. The "ambulance chasing" lawyer may pay a police officer for all referrals. Police officers, especially those who investigate traffic accidents, are in a good position to suggest an attorney for a possible liability suit. Towing companies and automobile repair and body shops are highly competitive businesses that can benefit from a good working relationship with one or more police officers. In fact, most police agencies have established a rotating list of wrecker services to avoid the possibility of corrupt arrangements.

Some police assignments have more potential for kickbacks than others. These include, for example, accident investigation, especially those units that investigate serious injuries and fatalities, which almost always result in civil litigation (lawyer-police conspiracy); complaint desk assignments (lawyer, bondsmen-police conspiracy); bond details (bondsmen-police conspiracy).

A Murfreesboro, Tennessee police officer admitted that he accepted money in exchange for sending business to towing companies and body shops. One towing company owner said: "To me the boy needed money. He was able to help me, so I helped him. He gave us jobs and I gave him cash. That's it." The last two sheriff's of Tunica County, Mississippi were convicted of taking kickbacks from bail bondsmen.

OPPORTUNISTIC THEFTS. These occur when police officers steal money or other valuables from those they stop, arrest, from crime victims, or property that comes into their possession. A Memphis police officer was sentenced to 27 months in prison for stealing money from three Hispanic drivers he pulled over (DOJ, 2009). A Customs and Border Protection Officer at the Philadelphia airport was convicted of stealing a laptop that was left in the customs area by an airline passenger.

Included in this pattern of corruption are thefts from crime scenes and unprotected property from victims. These behaviors do not involve corruptors. Corruption definitions that only deal with bribery miss the mark when discussing corrupt police behavior. The "rolled" arrestees, traffic accident victims, and unconscious or dead citizens are unaware of the corrupt act; there is no corruptor per se. A Miami, Florida officer responded to a traffic accident and transported the victim to the hospital in his patrol car. The officer found the victim's bankcard in his patrol car and persuaded the victim to give him his pin number. The officer then went to an ATM and withdrew $460.00.

Officers who engage in this behavior do not, in all likelihood, begin their shifts with the intention of stealing something; however, the opportunity presents itself under a low-risk situation and a theft occurs. I heard years ago that a good explanation of crime is, "Crime occurs when the opportunity and the inclination come together under a low-risk situation." This is a simple but true explanation for most rational acts of criminal behavior. The officers committing these acts already have the inclination; all they need is the opportunity and what they perceive to be a low-risk situation.

Perhaps an officer is called to or discovers a business that has been burglarized and decides to take some of the merchandise or money left behind by the first thief. On occasion, police officers have taken money or other valuables from unconscious or dead crime victims, particularly those involved in illegal activities, e.g., a drug dealer shot during a drug transaction. Thoroughly corrupt officers sometimes target innocent victims or natural death victims. Robert Leuci, bestselling author, retired New York City cop and admitted corrupt officer, in his book, *All the Centurions* (2004), describes the practice he observed of soaping down the fingers of dead persons to remove their rings. According to other officers I have interviewed over the years, this practice is (or was) common in other departments. Police officers making routine business checks may find a door unlocked or some other unsecured property and decide to take something.

Sometimes individuals who have a propensity for these acts are also well known. I have always advocated that police officers always know who the bad actors are in their departments. That is the really sad part of corruption control and management. I was teaching a class on police ethics some years ago when an officer made the comment, "We have an officer in our department who you would not want investigating a traffic accident that you or a member of your family was involved in." The implication being that he would take something from the victims, especially if they were dead or unconscious. Several other members of the class joined in and one even mentioned him by name. When I asked why they did not do something about him, they all replied, "Damn, Doc, you know why we don't." I sure did. They felt some strange sense of loyalty to this officer because he was a cop. They also did not want to be known as snitches. I told them that there were no honest cops watching dishonest cops commit crimes. I also told them that I believed that law enforcement would never be a profession as long as "some cops had their hands in other people's pockets and other cops knew about it and did nothing." I will return to this point later.

SHAKEDOWNS. This involves police officers extorting money or other valuables from criminals, usually caught in the act, or traffic violators. Law enforcement officers who enforce licensing regulation or collect taxes can also shakedown those they deal with. These forms of behavior often arise opportunistically, i.e., the officer inadvertently witnesses or gains knowledge of a criminal violation and violator and accepts a bribe for not making an arrest. Shakedowns are usually engaged in with little fear of being caught because the victims are unlikely to complain since they are engaged in some illegal activity. Two Chicago police officers were convicted of executing search warrants and making traffic stops on suspected drug dealers and then shaking them down in 2005 and 2006. One officer "ratted" out the other for a reduced sentence.

Officers will take bribes from transporters of contraband such as drugs, gambling paraphernalia or pornography, bootleg liquor or cigarettes; or traffic violators. Police officers have taken money or drugs from dealers caught in the act of transporting or dealing. The New York City's Police Department's "Buddy Boys" scandal is a good example of this pattern of corruption (McAlary, 1987). In a recent NYPD case, a nine-year veteran officer pulled over a drug courier and took $150,000 from him before letting him go (Dienst, 2009). The officer and long time friend were caught in an FBI sting when they agreed to transport 22 pounds of cocaine in the officer's patrol car for $15,000. A Phoenix, Arizona police officer was caught in a police sting after an arrested drug dealer told authorities that the officer was robbing drug dealers of money and releasing them without an arrest

(Ferraresi, 2010). Police investigators set up a traffic stop and tempted the officer with $40,000 of what was supposed to be drug money.

Today's police officer, particularly in a large urban city, may sooner or later be presented with a situation where he or she is exposed to temptations unheard of in the past. This has to be realized and discussed. All law enforcement officers must face the issues. We do not want them to face the temptations of huge sums of money without having some idea of what they might do or should do. Fortunately, most will make the right and ethical decision; however, some will yield to the temptation and a small number are waiting for the opportunity to arise. The latter group will seek out opportunities to shake down criminals and traffic violators.

In the area of traffic violators, virtually all uniformed police officers have numerous opportunities to shakedown those whom they stop for traffic offenses. The McIntosh County, Oklahoma sheriff and his undersheriff pleaded guilty to extorting money for motorists during traffic stops. Their last victim was an undercover FBI agent. A Lawtey, Florida police officer was arrested for charging a roadside fee for traffic violations (Anon f, 2010). He gave the stopped motorist three options: (1) contest it in court, (2) pay the fine and get four points on their license, or (3) pay the roadside fee and not get any points on their license. Illegal immigrants have become a particularly vulnerable target for shakedowns by corrupt officers. Cases have been reported in Mobile County, Alabama (Kramer, 2010). The serious consequences associated with DUI arrests and convictions have introduced a new potential for corrupt activities.

COSTS OF A DUI SHAKEDOWN

INTOXICATED DRIVER PAYS OFFICER $100 TO FORGET VIOLATION

COST TO THE CITY — Loss of fine, loss of credibility in traffic enforcement. Damage to city's reputation. Amount of future shakedowns, increased likelihood that he will be stopped in future, possibility of being prosecuted, increased risk of death and injury.
COSTS TO THE DRIVER — Increased risk of death or injury from released offender, increased likelihood they will be stopped in hopes they can be shaken down for a bribe.

COSTS TO THE PUBLIC — Increased risks of death and injury, increased insurance rates, justice only for those who can pay.
COSTS TO POLICE AGENCY — Damage to reputation, loss of confidence in agency, loss of individual officer's credibility.

Certain individuals and businesses are particularly vulnerable to shakedowns, because they are subject to local, state, and federal licensing regulations. A Pennsylvania State Liquor Enforcement Officer pleaded guilty to nine counts of Hobbs Act extortion for using her official position to obtain money from the owners of bars (DOJ, June, 2010). Law enforcement officers in agencies at all levels of government that enforce tax collections are in a position to extort bribes. An IRS agent has been charged with soliciting and accepting a bribe from two businesses that owed taxes (DOJ j, June 3, 2010). It is alleged that the agent agreed to lie about their audit to make what they owed more manageable. The businessmen taped the first conversation and then turned the agent over to law enforcement which taped the second conversation and provided the bribe money.

PROTECTION OF ILLEGAL ACTIVITIES. This refers to those forms of behavior where law enforcement officers receive protection money or other valuables from vice operators or legitimate companies that operate illegally. Operators of so-called victimless crimes, including vice operations related to gambling, illegal drug sales, prostitution, liquor violations, pornography rings, and after-hours clubs, can increase their profits and decrease their risks through a good working relationship with the police. Five Prince George, Maryland police were recently accused of working security for a high-stakes gambling ring involving drug dealers. All of the accused officers resigned or retired. Recently, in Georgia, a Fulton County deputy sheriff was indicted for providing armed protection to drug dealers. Unfortunately, there has been a long history of collusion between police and vice operations in many American cities. The new border restrictions after 9/11 have opened up new avenues for opportunities. A Customs and Border Protection officer working at the Brownsville, Texas Port of Entry was recently arrested for alien smuggling and drug charges. Allegedly the officer allowed vehicles carrying aliens, cocaine, or sometimes both through his lane.

A Pennsylvania state trooper pleaded guilty to charges of obstruction and impeding the administration of justice for tipping off pimps who ran a nationwide prostitution ring (DOJ, 2008; Scolforo, 2008).

The trooper was assigned to anti-prostitution patrols at a truck stop near Harrisburg, Pennsylvania. A prostitution ring, primarily out of Toledo, Ohio, was operating out of the truck stop. At least 125 prostitutes, nine under age 18, operated out of the truck stop. The officer received sex and money for his corrupt acts. One pimp even let him have sex with his prostitute for arresting a competitor. He warned the pimps and prostitutes about undercover operations, law enforcement wiretaps, and sweeps. The trooper even provided copies of his work schedule to let them know that they would not be arrested during the time he worked.

Protection money or goods can also come from legitimate companies that operate illegally. Law enforcement officers have control over numerous businesses that are restricted by license and the law. For example, taxicabs, restaurants, trucking firms, bars, liquor stores, pharmacies, pawnshops, and gun dealers are among those regulated by law. These types of companies or businesses, some more than others, have paid tribute to the police to operate outside the range of their licenses or other restrictions; for example, a bar that stays open after hours or serves liquor or food for which it does not have a license or a taxicab that operates outside prescribed routes or picks up or discharges fares at unauthorized sites.

There has also been a long tradition in some urban cities of construction companies paying police officers to overlook violations of city regulations, e.g., trucks blocking traffic, violating pollution guidelines, and blocking sidewalks.

The increased specialization brought about by attempts to professionalize police departments has created a situation where it is not necessary to pay off all members of an entire police organization to insure protection. Only the detail that handles the relevant activity – cab detail, drug unit, vice detail, etc. – must be paid off.

FIXES. There are two behavior patterns included within the **fix**: the quashing of misdemeanor or felony prosecutions and the disposal of traffic tickets. This form of bribery involves the officer taking something of value to fix a case or a traffic ticket. Obviously, it would be easier for the uniformed officer to fix a misdemeanor case than a felony case. He or she would have more control over misdemeanor cases or tickets. In a felony prosecution, a detective or someone from the prosecutor's office would handle the matter. The detective/s would be in a better position for a felony fix. Prior to or at the preliminary hearing is the optimum period to fix a criminal case. Should the case proceed to the grand jury or trial court stage, it becomes more difficult and more expensive to fix a case. When the "fix is in," the investigating officer agrees to "sell the case," that is, withdraw prosecution. He or she fails to request prosecution, tampers with the existing evidence, or gives perjured testimony. He or she can also say that they failed to do something that they were required to do, such as giving the **Miranda Warning** or securing a search warrant.

I sadly recall when I had about two years on the job; two drunken young men stepped out of a "protected" whisky house and tried to shoot me off a three-wheeled police motorcycle. They fired at least five times as I frantically called for help. Police cars in a matter of minutes saturated the area. The two suspects were found hiding under a house. While we were waiting for trial, I was told that the detectives handling the case were going to "sell it." I went to my sergeant, who later became a "reform" chief renowned for his "honesty" and told him what I had heard. He told me "there is no way they would fix a case of attempted murder on a cop." The case went to trial without notifying me and the suspects pleaded guilty to the charge of discharging a firearm in the city limits. The attempted murder charge was reduced for $600. I went to my sergeant and complained and he said, "There ain't nothing I can do, that's the way things are around here." I have told this story at training sessions and have been told that nothing like that would happen again. I hope they are right.

It is becoming more and more difficult to fix traffic tickets as states move to serially numbered uniform traffic citations. There has to be some explanation given for a missing or rescinded ticket. Nevertheless, this has not stopped ticket fixing by some officers. In 2009, a Dearborn, Michigan police officer was arrested for running a traffic fixing scheme for years. The officer recovered tickets written by other officers and fixed them for money.

DIRECT CRIMINAL ACTIVITIES. All forms of police corruption are serious ethical violations and crimes; however, this pattern of behavior is particularly grave. Police officers actively engage in such crimes as robbery, burglary, the sale and trafficking in narcotics, or other criminal conspiracies in this pattern. These officers are crooks in uniform. When I first began conducting research on police corruption, I would never have believed that law enforcement officers would become involved in drug-related corruption as some have today.

Drug-related corruption has changed the nature of police corruption. Police officers involved in drug-related corruption are more likely to operate on their own or in small groups and to be involved in a variety of crimes such as stealing drugs and money from drug dealers, selling drugs, and lying under oath during illegal searches (U.S. Government Accounting Office, 1998: 3). Rotten apples involved in drug-related corruption have appeared in all levels of police agencies. In 2009, a veteran FBI special agent was convicted of conspiracy to commit a robbery affecting interstate commerce, interstate travel to commit a crime of violence with a firearm, possession of a firearm in furtherance of a crime of violence, and possession of a machine gun (DOJ, 2009). The agent and an accomplice who had police experience traveled from New Orleans to Fountain Valley, California to commit a home invasion on a drug stash house operated by a drug trafficking organization and filled with drugs and cash. In California, they met with two other men to plan the home invasion. Unbeknownst to the two conspirators, the two men they met with were an undercover FBI agent and a civilian working with the FBI. The corrupt agent had plans to put together a small crew to commit home invasions of drug dealers in southern California. An ATF special agent was indicted for conspiracy to distribute methamphetamine, cocaine, and marijuana, possessing methamphetamines with intent to distribute, possessing a firearm during drug trafficking and money laundering (Terribone, 2010). He pleaded guilty to conspiring to distribute more than 50 grams of methamphetamine. This ATF special agent also conspired with a municipal officer to frame innocent subjects and will be discussed later.

A Massachusetts state trooper pleaded guilty and was sentenced to 37 months in prison for conspiring to possess and distribute oxycodone and cocaine (DOJ, 2009). A South Carolina sheriff is under arrest and waiting trial for allegedly selling drugs from his police vehicle and using a list of possible drug dealers from another state officer to tip them off and extort money from them (AP b, May, 3, 2010). A New York City police detective was sentenced to 15 years in prison for distributing narcotics (DOJ, 2010). He assisted the operation of a cocaine and crack enterprise by warning the distributor of impending police actions and providing information from law enforcement databases. A Laredo, Texas International Airport police officer pleaded guilty and was sentenced to 20 months in federal prison for selling cocaine while in uniform at the airport (DOJ, 2009). He sold cocaine to a cooperative FBI source four times, all monitored by the FBI.

Rotten apples have come together in corrupt groups and are more likely to involve themselves in shakedowns of drug users or dealers, or robberies of dealers and crack houses. They are real badge-packing criminals. New York City's former Police Commissioner William Bratton, commenting on the Mollen Commission's findings, stated, "we have criminals in blue uniforms who are more vicious than some of the criminals they are supposedly policing" (Bratton, 1995: 39). Certainly, the so-called NYPD "Mafia Cops" fit what Commissioner Bratton was talking about. The two retired detectives were convicted of directly participating in, or aiding and abetting, eight murders, two attempted murders, and one murder conspiracy for the Luchese crime family while employed with the NYPD (DOJ, 2009). Their 2006 conviction was overturned because of statute of limitations issues and the judgment was reversed. They were sentenced to life in prison without parole.

A three-man criminal crew of "badge-packing criminals" led by Boston Police Officer Roberto Pulido was involved in identity theft, wire fraud, steroid smuggling, assault and battery, framing an innocent man and running illegal stripper parties (DOJ, 2008). The FBI and the Boston Police Department set up an undercover operation offering the corrupt cops the opportunity to protect three large shipments of cocaine. The officers took money and protected the three shipments, one involving 100 kilograms. Pulido, after pleading guilty, received 26 years in prisons. His co-conspirators received 13 and 18 years respectfully.

A recent example of "criminals in blue uniforms" occurred in the Memphis, Tennessee Police Department with the conviction of former officer Arthur Sease IV (DOJ, 2009). Sease was convicted of 44 counts of civil rights, narcotics, robbery, and firearms offenses and sentenced to life plus 255 years in prison. Sease and his crew of officers, at least three, robbed suspected drug dealers of cash, cocaine, and marijuana. They would then sell the drugs for their own profit. The corrupt police crew was involved in 15 separate robberies.

Carter (1990) reports that his police subjects involved in drug corruption gave interesting rationalization for their stealing from or robbing drug dealers. They would not take bribes; that was corruption. However, stealing from and robbing drug users and dealers did not "hurt anyone except the criminals" (p. 91). I have heard the same rationalization on several occasions, sometimes during ethics training sessions: "Its not corruption when you're taking it from the dirt bags."

All the criminals in blue uniforms are not males. Sergeant Shanita McKnight of the Lake City, South Carolina Police Department was sentenced to 20 years for extortion and drug conspiracy (DOJ, 2009). She was a co-owner of a nightclub run by her mother and aunt where crack cocaine was sold and smoked and prostitutes were available. She also warned her family and other drug dealers about police activity in the area. She was present when drugs were sold and used and took no action. Lake City PD was a corrupt police department in a corrupt city. A female, NYPD, 11-year veteran officer pleaded guilty to conspiring to rob drug dealers. She conspired with her uncle to rob the drug dealers. The uncle "flipped" on her after being caught and wore a wire for the police.

Police officers have stolen drugs from evidence storage areas and sold it themselves or in conspiracies with other officers or coconspirators. A detective-sergeant with the Passaic County, New Jersey Sheriff's Department was sentenced to 85 months in federal prison for stealing 43 kilograms of cocaine and 700 grams of heroin from the department's evidence vault (DOJ, 2009). Included within the officer's duty was supervising the destruction of seized drugs. The officer received at least $250,000 from the sale of the drugs.

In 2008, three Indianapolis Metro police officers were found guilty of possessing with intent to distribute 50 kilograms of marijuana. In 2009, 28 defendants were arrested in Texas and California for operating a major methamphetamine operation since 2003 in west Texas, Ari-zona, and Modesto, California. Two of those indicted were Hockley County, Texas deputy sheriffs.

Badge-packing criminals commit crimes not directly related to drugs. Two NYPD officers conspired with five others, including a former NYPD officer, to rob a perfume warehouse of approximately $600,000 worth of perfume (DOJ, 2010). The group entered the warehouse brandishing weapons, displaying NYPD-issued badges, and announcing themselves as NYPD officers. They restrained 11 employees with flex cuffs and held them hostage while they loaded the boxes into rental trucks. Proving that criminal cops are often no smarter than any other criminals, one of the cops used his own ATM debit card to rent the trucks.

A 22-year veteran officer of the Conroe, Texas Police Department was convicted of robbing the First Bank of Conroe (DOJ, 2010). In another incident of pure stupidity, the officer had worked security for the bank for 19 years. Bank employees recognized his voice, mannerisms, gait, and clothing even though he wore a motorcycle helmet. During the robbery, the heavily in debt officer used terms only understood by bank insiders.

The large influx of illegal immigrants has created new opportunities for corrupt behavior and criminal conspiracies. A criminal conspiracy case investigated by 17 law enforcement agencies, including federal, state, and local police in Massachusetts and New Hampshire led to the arrest of a New Hampshire state trooper and a Division of Motor Vehicle employee (Barrick, 2010; Bencks, 2010; Cote, 2009). The DMV employee supplied driver's licenses based on fake identities and Social Security to an immigrant from the Dominican Republic who in turn sold them to illegal immigrants. The trooper supplied inspection stickers for cars that had been totaled or stolen and recovered. The DMV employee received $500 for each license.

Increased homeland security created by 9/11 provided new criminal opportunities for federal agents, local police, correctional officers, military personnel, and government employees responsible for issuing passports, visas, and green cards (FBI, 05/17/2010). In May 2010, a former U.S. Customs officer was sentenced to 19 months in prison for stamping the immigration documents of a French citizen without running his name through government databases (AP, 2010). The Customs officer received a $4,800 bribe for his actions. A U.S. Immigration and Customs Enforcement (ICE) deportation officer pleaded guilty to obstructions of justice and producing a fraudulent immigration document (DOJ, 2009). The ICE agent shredded the files of two aliens awaiting deportation. A Customs and Border Protection Officer was sentenced to 37 months in prison allowing illegal aliens to be smuggled through his line at the San Luis Port of Entry in San Luis, Arizona and accepting a bribe (DOJ, 2010). The agent collaborated with smugglers who charged a fee and then split it with the agent. In 2009, a Border Patrol Agent was indicted for accepting bribes from drug traffickers. He took $1000 from a drug trafficker for a law enforcement sensitive map showing roads, trails, and landmarks used by the Border Patrol. On two other occasions, he accepted money for a list of sensors in the Sonoita, Arizona area. These criminal behaviors are particularly troubling and represent a serious threat to the homeland.

Potential Threat to the Homeland

- A corrupt officer might believe that he or she is accepting a bribe in return for allowing a carload of illegal immigrants to enter the country, when those individuals may actually be hard-core gang members or terrorists.
- A crooked official who expedites someone's immigration paperwork or helps someone obtain an identification document in return for a bribe could potentially be facilitating the operation of a terrorist cell, foreign counterintelligence network, or major criminal enterprise.
- A corrupt officer could knowingly or unknowingly allow entry of a truck, rail car, ship, or airplane carrying weapons of mass destruction, chemical or biological weapons, or bomb-making materials (FBI, 2010).

In order to meet these potential threats, the Federal Bureau of Investigation (FBI) has created several FBI-led Border Corruption Task Forces composed of representatives from the FBI; Department of Homeland Security agencies, including Customs and Border Protection Internal Affairs, Transportation Security Administration, Immigration and Customs Enforcement, and Department of Homeland Security – Office of Inspector General. The task forces also included representatives from state and local law enforcement agencies. The task forces were first set up along the southwest border and are now also in Detroit, Miami, and San Juan. Task forces are planned for Buffalo, Newark, and Seattle.

A Santa Cruz, Arizona deputy sheriff was terminated after his indictment for allegedly transporting cocaine through the I–19 checkpoint in uniform while driving his marked patrol car (DOJ Press Release, May 5, 2010). Since he was in uniform and carrying his service weapon, the deputy was also indicted for possessing a firearm in furtherance of a drug trafficking crime. The Southern Arizona Border Corruption Task Force made the arrest.

INTERNAL PAYOFFS. This is a unique form of police corruption because the corruptors and the corruptees are both law enforcement officers. Police officers "sell" work assignments, off-days, holidays, evidence, influence, and promotions to each other. An officer would approach his or her supervisor and request a change in work assignment and suggest a money figure, or the supervisor might tell the officer how much such a change would cost. Officers who work in departmental records may sell confidential information to other officers. A Chicago police officer is accused of extorting money from a fellow officer to influence the Chicago Police Board that oversees disciplinary actions (Anon, May 10, 2010). The suspect officer was facing serious disciplinary trouble when he was approached by the accused officer who said he could "put the fix" in for $10,000. The suspect officer offered to act as an undercover agent for the FBI who recorded the conversations between the two officers.

Internal payoffs could involve department's selling positions. In 1995, a federal grand jury reviewed FBI reports concerning allegations that applicants to the Shelby County, Tennessee Sheriff's Office were asked to pay as much as $7,000 to obtain jobs as deputies (*Law Enforcement News*, September 30, 1995: 51). Evidence or records would probably be sold for use in some other pattern of corruption, such as a **shakedown** or **protection of illegal activities**.

For such transactions as **internal payoffs** to occur, both parties would, in all probability, have to be already involved in some corrupt practices. In all likelihood, the work assignment sold would be one with a high corruption potential. I feel confident that **internal payoffs** are the rarest form of police corruption because police officers are the victims and **internal payoffs** would only occur in departments riddled with the other patterns of corruption.

Chapter 9

CORRUPT PRACTICES AND CORRUPTION CONTROL

If we are to understand and control corrupt behavior, we must recognize that corrupt practices will vary according to their organization and officer involvement. Patterns representing adventitious corruption are not organized since they occur opportunistically. Other patterns such as **protection of illegal activities** are highly organized (see Table 9–1).

Opportunistic events such as "scores" are most often one-time events that are never repeated between the same officer and a citizen, victim, or criminal. Other corrupt activities feature a continuing relationship among parties to the corruption. There will be active cooperation between officers. There can also be passive cooperation among officers when "honest" officers do not report their colleagues. There will also be citizen-police cooperation, particularly in vice operations. The length of time that this cooperation takes place will also vary. Obviously, the longer the length of cooperation, the more serious the problem.

Corrupt Officers and Corrupt Groups: "Rotten Apples"

The traditional view and the one most often expressed by police executives in the past was that police corruption was the result of a few **rotten apples** in an otherwise honest police department. These rotten apples were either weak individuals who had slipped through the screening process and succumbed to the temptations inherent in police work, or deviant individuals who continue their deviant practices in an environment of ample opportunity.

Table 9-1. PATTERNS OF POLICE CORRUPTION.

Pattern	Acts	Organization
Kickbacks	Money or money's worth from those who service the clients of the police.	High, collusion between corruptors and the police.
Opportunistic Thefts	Thefts from arrestees, victims, crime scenes, and unprotected property.	None
Shakedowns	Money, goods or other valuables from criminals or traffic offenders.	None
Protection of Illegal Activities	Protection money from vice operators or companies operating illegally.	High: often highly organized.
Fixes	Quashing of prosecution proceedings or companies operating illegally.	Medium; fixers could be on the payroll.
Direct Criminal Activities	Officers engaged in such crimes as burglary, robbery, sale and trafficking in drugs, border smuggling.	Low for some crimes – burglary, robberies – small groups. Medium to high organization in drugs and smuggling.
Internal Payoffs	Sale of work assignments, off-days, evidence, and promotions.	Low to high; depending on other forms of corruption present.

As we have stated, the very nature of this morally dangerous occupation provides its members with more than ample opportunity to engage in a wide variety of deviant behaviors, including corruption. The police come into contact with a variety of deviant actors during their normal work routine, often under conditions of little or no supervision.

The temptations, coupled with the discretion that the officer can and does exercise, makes police work much more morally dangerous than any other occupation.

The Knapp Commission, which investigated the New York City corruption scandal in the early 1970s, was the first to identify two types of officers who could qualify as rotten apples: grass eaters and meat eaters (Knapp Commission, 1973). **Grass Eaters** are officers who engage in relatively minor types of corruption as the opportunity presents itself. **Meat Eaters**, on the other hand, are police officers who actively seek out corruption opportunities and engage in both minor and major patterns of corruption. Typically patterns engaged in by the **meat eaters** are kickbacks, opportunistic thefts, shakedowns, fixes, and direct criminal activities.

The police corruption scandals of the 1970s and 1980s, including the Knapp Commission, provided little support for the rotten apple theory, as systematic corruption was found in department after department (Barker & Carter, 1994). The problem was the barrel and not the apples. The term "rotten apple" came to be seen as a management technique or rationalizations used by police executives to explain corrupt behavior in their departments. They were trying to use this label to normalize or distance the police department from one or more publicly identified corrupt police officers.

It now appears that changes in departmental control systems in the last 15 to 20 years have had an effect on the nature of police corrupt practices in many police departments. Hugo Masini, former chief and the first director of the Institute for Criminal Justice Ethics, states that, before the administration of New York City Police Commissioner Patrick Murphy, there had never been a "clear-cut" message in the department that corruption would not be tolerated and that officers and supervisors would be held accountable for it (Masini, 1985: iv). This was to take place in other departments. The systematic corruption scandals of the 1970s and 1980s led to administrative changes in most major police departments. There is now reason to revisit the rotten apple explanation.

ROTTEN APPLES REVISITED. Many writers and researchers on this topic, the author included, may have gone too far in dismissing rotten apples as an explanation of some corrupt police behavior. It is now apparent that rotten apples do occur in many police departments. A true rotten apple is a corrupt officer in a police department where systematic corruption is truly rare (Barker, 1996: 39). The rotten apple argument has been confirmed in many police departments (Delattre, 1989). For example, Delattre is correct in pointing out that the River Cops involved in the drug corruption scandal in Miami, Florida in the late 1980s were rotten apples in a department without evidence of systematic corruption. The River Cops were hired during a period of accelerated hiring and relaxed standards for employment (more on this issue later).

The Mollen Commission's investigation – the sixth commission to investigate corruption in New York since 1890 – of drug corruption in the New York City Police Department arrived at the same conclusion: "The corrupt acts were the result of small groups of rotten apples and not systematic corruption within the department" (Mollen Commission, 1994.) I am not aware of any evidence to discredit this conclusion. However, as in Miami, management and supervisory deficiencies, including the failure to support a sergeant who reported the corrupt acts in New York, contributed to the problem (McAlary, 1994).

The investigation into the Los Angeles Rampart Area corruption incident appears to be the result of rotten apples and not corruption throughout the department (Los Angeles Police Department, 2000). There does not appear to be any evidence to dispute this finding. Although numerous management and supervisory deficiencies contributed to corrupt acts and the abuses of authority, it appears that the corruption was limited to the corrupt acts of a Rampart CRASH (specialized gang) unit. The unit had a gunfighter attitude and a siege mentality. One could also argue that the unit's name, CRASH, is confrontational.

LAPD Board of Inquiry

> After careful consideration of the information developed during the Board of Inquiry's work, it is the Board's view that the Rampart corruption incident occurred because a few individuals decided to engage in blatant misconduct and, in some cases, criminal behavior. Published assertions by former Rampart CRASH officer Rafael Perez that the pressure to produce arrests caused him to become corrupt, simply ignores the fact that he was convicted of stealing narcotics so he could sell them and live the life style of a "high roller." Even the finest corruption prevention system will not stop an individual from committing a crime if he or she has the will to do so. However, had the Department and the Rampart management exercised more vigorous and coordinated oversight of Area operations, and its CRASH unit in particular, the crimes and misconduct that occurred may have been prevented, discouraged, or discovered much earlier. (Los Angeles Police Department, 2000: 311)

The recent Chicago drug corruption scandal also was confined to specialized units. The ten Chicago officers indicted were tactical unit officers whose primary function was narcotics enforcement. They were assigned to the two districts with the highest incidents of narcotics arrests (Commission on Police Integrity, 1997).

From all accounts, the 1999 charge of police corruption in the Seattle Police Department was limited to one police detective accused of stealing $10,000 from the home of a man who died in a police shootout (SPD Citizens Review Panel, 1999: 1). Significantly, a Seattle Homicide Detective reported the incident to a county deputy prosecutor, even though the original detective returned the money at the urging of his colleagues on the scene. The single allegation in a department with a national reputation for being corruption free led the mayor to convene a citizen's panel to investigate the incident.

There is no denying that the evidence does suggest that rotten apples do exist. However, some police executives still use the term rotten apples to deny or mask problems in their departments. They want the public to believe that a publicly identified corrupt, or for that matter, a racist or brutal cop is an aberration not a department problem. When they are gone, the problem will go away. Generally speaking, rotten apples are uncovered internally by fellow police officers. In a truly honest police organization, especially one that has a proactive internal affairs division, corrupt officers – or racist and brutal officers – will soon be identified. However, in those departments with rotten apples, if they are left unattended to they will soon come together and practice their deviant activities in groups. If individual police officers engage in corrupt practices for any length of time without the department discovering it or taking action, if they know of it, it is almost inevitable that they will become known to each other and begin to act in collusion. These officers will begin to organize for corrupt activities. In time, corrupt practices can become widespread and lead to corrupt police departments. But first we need to examine relaxed hiring standards and its effects on hiring potential rotten apples.

RELAXED HIRING STANDARDS. Particularly troubling about the Los Angeles Police Department's Rampart Investigation is that four of the 14 officers (12 men and 2 women) involved were hired during periods of accelerated hiring and were disqualified by the police department only to be hired by the personnel department (LAPD, 2000: 332). During the background checks, the police department learned that four police officer applicants had a combination of criminal records, inability to manage personal finances, histories of violent behavior, or narcotics involvement. One had sold narcotics as a juvenile. Nevertheless, the personnel department, which had the final say on employment, overruled the police department. This is not the first time that a link has been found between relaxed hiring practices and police corruption and misconduct.

In 1980, Miami, Florida, under pressure to recruit minority candidates, adopted a policy that 200 new police officers be hired immediately. Eight percent of these new recruits were to come from the minority community. Little, if any background checks were conducted on these new applicants. In addition, these new recruits were badly trained and negligently supervised. The background checks that were done and the police academy instructor's reports revealed that many were unsuited for police work. The end result was that by 1988, a third were fired and 12 members of the group known as the "River Cops" were convicted of crimes ranging from drug trafficking to murder. Many had joined the department to engage in drug trafficking.

During the 1989–90 hiring drive in Washington, D.C., numerous officers who were to become problem officers were hired under relaxed standards and background checks. Congress threatened to withhold $430 million unless 1,800 new officers were hired. The Metropolitan Police Department hired 1,471 officers in 1989 and 1990. In order to accomplish this, the department suspended the normal procedures for applications and lowered the passing grade on the entrance exam to 50 percent. Background checks were done over the phone and FBI criminal records were ignored. Delattre (1995) reports that some of the applicants were incarcerated at the time and they received their parole denial letters at the same time that they received notices that they were admitted to the police academy.

By 1997, one hundred of the officers hired under the relaxed standards had been charged with criminal offenses ranging from shoplifting to rape and murder. One hundred of these officers are included in the 185 Metro officers who cannot be used as credible witnesses because of their bad records. One-quarter of the total number had been charged with crimes involving domestic abuse (Human Rights Watch, 1998). The special committee appointed to examine the allegations of misconduct recommended that the Metropolitan Police Department be prohibited from hiring an applicant without a full background check, including a review of juvenile records (www.dcwatch.com/police/981006a.htm#introduction: 6 & 7).

A most disturbing example of the consequences of hiring the wrong person occurred in New Orleans in 1995. On-duty Officer Antoinette Frank and an accomplice entered a Vietnamese restaurant, killed an off-duty police officer moonlighting as a security guard, and then executed a brother and sister who worked in the family business. Frank later answered the call to the restaurant as if nothing had happened. Officer Frank received the death penalty for the murders. In 1993, Frank had failed the civil service psychiatric evaluation and hired her own psychiatrist, who found her fit. A second civil service psychiatrist evaluated the contradictory evaluations and declared her suitable for employment as a New Orleans police officer (Human Rights Watch, 1998).

A more recent example of relaxed hiring practices translating into the hiring of rotten apples may be occurring with the push to hire more agents for the Department of Homeland Security, particularly Customs and Border Enforcement agents. A *New York Times* article reports that there has been a 40 percent increase in arrests accompanying the 24 percent increase in the size of the agency (Archibold, 2009). During the hiring boom, traffickers are soliciting their own operatives to apply for the jobs. The operatives without criminal records were encouraged to apply because they could pass the background checks. At the time the article was published only 10 percent of the applicants were given a polygraph screening because of a lack of funds to conduct the screening. New hires were allowed to serve in the areas they grew up in because of relaxed restrictions to increase recruiting. This increases the risk of family and peer pressure on the new recruits.

The failure of the internal discipline system may result in identified rotten apples staying in a police department. Carter (1990) reports the case of a police officer who was confiscating drugs for his own use. To avoid bad press, the department charged the officer with a departmental rule violation instead of a crime. The department hoped to fire the officer. The officer's due process rights were violated during the process, and a later arbitrator put the officer back to work with most of his back pay. This same officer was later promoted to sergeant. It is not uncommon for arbitrators to overturn department disciplinary decisions (Coulson, 1993).

The combined effect of these practices – relaxed hiring practices, hiring the wrong person when evidence of their unsuitability is available, failure of the internal discipline system, or no such system – can lead to employing or retaining rotten apples. Rotten apples can form corrupt groups and over time lead to corrupt departments.

Corrupt Police Departments

In this case, a sizable number, if not the majority, of the police officers in some police departments engage in corrupt activities. The most extreme example of a corrupt police department would be a department that adopts corrupt goals. This occurs when the department is "captured" by the political environment or the "dominant coalition" adopts personal gain as a goal (Sherman, 1978: 32). The author had the unfortunate experience of working in such a department. Corrupt police departments exist today.

We earlier examined the current problems of the New Orleans Police Department and the allegations from the leading newspaper that NOPD is the most inefficient and most corrupt police department in the nation. The newly elected mayor has asked for federal help in cleaning up the department. Other examples exist.

The chief of the nine-officer Sullivan City, Texas Police Department near the Mexican border was indicted for conspiracy to distribute marijuana – more than 1,000 kilograms – and four counts of possession with intent to distribute between 100 kilograms and 1,000 kilograms of marijuana (Perez, 2010). The chief was one of the 2,000 persons arrested during Operation Deliverance, a two-year, multiagency operation in 16 states against the Mexican drug cartels (Roebuck, 2010). Following the beating death of an illegal Mexican immigrant, four members of the seven-member Shenandoah, Pennsylvania Police Department were indicted and arrested for obstructing the investigation of the fatal assault, witness and evidence tampering and lying to the FBI, multiple counts of extortion, and civil rights violations (DOJ-Office of Public Affairs, 2009). The extortion charges included attempts to extort cash payments from illegal gambling operations in the Shenandoah area and demanding a $2,000 cash payment from a local businessman to release him from custody. The chief was denied bail and ordered jailed after his arrest and the other three officers were released on home confinement (Kalinowski, 2009). The judge, in denying bail to the chief, said, "[you] represent a threat to the community, witnesses and the integrity of the law enforcement system." All four of the officers resigned from the department.

The state of New Jersey has a long history of official corruption and several police departments, including West New York and Camden, had corruption scandals recently. In 1999, 30 West New York officers were charged with corruption-related offenses. The chief testified in court that the police department was a racketeering gang that accepted bribes and kickbacks to shield a prostitution ring, illicit liquor sales, and illegal gambling operations (Anon n, 1999). He admitted to collecting at least $2 million from loan-sharking and illegal gambling operations that he distributed to other officers involved. At the present time, the Camden PD is under investigation by the FBI for corrupt activities. Prosecutors say that some residents claim the police are worse than criminals and have bullied citizens for years, making cases by planting drugs, falsifying police reports, and conducting searches without warrants (Mulvihill, 2010). One officer has already pleaded guilty and admitted 50 to 70 acts of misconduct from May 2007 to October 2009. The actions of these corrupt officers will be discussed further under **Convicting the Innocent**.

As discussed earlier, former Sergeant Shanita McKnight of the Lake City, South Carolina Police Department was convicted and sentenced to 20 years for extortion and drug conspiracy and represents the example of corrupt police department in a corrupt city (see Timeline, Lake City, South Carolina Corruption).

Timeline
Lake City, South Carolina Corruption

Feb. 15, 2005 – Lake City Police Lt. William Webb arrested on federal drug charges of conspiracy with intent to distribute powder and/or crack cocaine. Lt. Webb's arrest resulted from an ongoing federal investigation into corruption and drug activity in the Lake City area.

June 29, 2005 – Sgt. McKnight and two Lake City police officers have their state police certifications suspended after failing polygraph tests in connection with the federal investigation.

July 6, 2005 – The Lake City Police Chief Kenneth McCaster who has been on the job for six months is fired by Lake City Administer George Simmons. Simmons says that he fired the chief because he wanted to fire the officers who failed the polygraph exams and he, Simmons, would not let him.

July 8, 2005 – Former Chief McCaster issues a public letter to the citizens explaining his firing and alleges that Lake City is "a thug-run city" and "a society of illegal administrative practices, sexual relations at work, political favors, nepotism, voter fraud, election fraud, intimidation, bad judicial (court practices), ticket fixing mixed with political pressure and favoritism and defiance and arrogance concerning other law enforcement agencies."

August 8, 2005 – State Law Enforcement Division agents take Sergeant McKnight into custody.

August 9, 2005 – Sgt. McKnight is officially charged with acceptance of money to conceal an offense involving a felony, misconduct in office, misprison of a felony, and obstruction of justice.

October 3, 2005 – Lt. Webb pleads guilty to one count of conspiracy to distribute crack cocaine and agrees to cooperate in the investigation of corruption.

January 2, 2006 – A South Carolina Law Enforcement Division (SLED) lieutenant takes the job as Lake City Police Chief.

January 11, 2006 – The new chief resigns after a week and returns to work as a SLED lieutenant.

February 16, 2006 – Former Lt. Webb is sentenced to 13 years and 4 months in prison.

April 19, 2006 – Mayor LaRue Alford is arrested on charges on misconduct in office and obstruction of justice. The arrest is the result of a 14-month investigation by the Florence County Sheriff's Office, SLED, the FBI, and the U.S. Secret Service.

April 29, 2006 – Mayor Alford is charged with dealing in counterfeit money.

May 9, 2006 – Lake City Administer George Simmons has his contract terminated. [He is the one who fired Chief McCaster for wanting to fire the officers when they failed the polygraph exams. Remember that McCaster said that the city was "thug run."]

July 27, 2006 – George Simmons is arrested on 19 counts of embezzlement of public funds and one count of misconduct in office.

November 2, 2006 – Simmons and former Lake City finance director Juanita Cunningham Bradley-Wragg are arrested for one count of mail fraud, conspiracy to commit mail fraud and program fraud, which relates to taking federal funding for personal use.

March 1, 2007 – An Assistant U.S. District Attorney adds 21 charges to the original indictment of Simmons and Bradley-Wragg.

March 5, 2007 – Former Mayor Alford pleads guilty to possession of counterfeit currency.

May 30, 2007 – Simmons and Bradley-Wragg finalize plea agreements. Simmons pleads guilty to three counts and Cunningham pleads to two.

June 1, 2007 – Alford is sentenced to five months in federal prison and three years of supervised release.

June 4, 2007 – Former Sgt. McKnight and her aunt are indicted on drug trafficking charges.

December 13, 2007 – Bradley-Wragg is sentenced to four months in prison, four months' house arrest, and three years supervised release.

March 19, 2008 – Simmons is sentenced to 51 months in prison on each of the three counts to run concurrently followed by three years supervision.

October 21, 2008 – Shanita McKnight is convicted of drug trafficking and extortion.

May 27, 2009 – McKnight is sentenced to 20 years on each count to run concurrently.

(Rogers, 2009).

In what may be an example of a corrupt police department, the two members of the drug unit for the Benton Harbor, Michigan Police Department were sent to prison for falsifying search-warrant affidavits, embezzling police funds, illegally seizing suspects' money and property, and conspiracy to violate civil rights (DOJ, 2009; Melzer a., 2009; Melzer b., 2009). The officers admitted to the charges. When drugs were found, the officers kept them for their own use and sale. To date, 40 drug cases have been dismissed. There are allegations that other officers are involved and that drugs were planted on innocent victims, an example of Noble Cause Injustice. The 20-officer police department of Spring Lake, North Carolina was disbanded and the sheriff's department took over all law enforcement duties when two officers were arrested on corruption charges and the chief resigned after being accused of shredding files (Heffernan, 2009; Mims, 2009). The county district attorney dismissed all pending misdemeanor cases because he suspected that senior police officers lied and directed other officers to fabricate facts in police reports.

All the patterns of corruption would be found in a corrupt police organization if the opportunities are present. Those patterns involving vice operations will predominate. Even though a sizable number of the officers will engage in corrupt activities, not all will do so. There are actually five categories of officers who can possibly exist in a department depending on the corruption present (Barker, 1986). The five categories are ideal types that exist along a continuum of behaviors, so that gradations of officers will fit in between.

Types of Officers in Police Organizations, Depending on the Corruption Present

1. WHITE KNIGHTS. These officers are honest to a fault or at least they say they are. They often take an extreme position on ethical issues. Although police officers are expected to be ethical and moral in their behavior, white knights can create problems in an organization by being too rigid and judgmental in an occupation that requires discretionary decision-making. I was always told to be wary of anyone who takes an extreme position on any issue. Often, those who take extreme positions, and they are usually vocal about it, are trying to convince themselves. Honest and ethical persons do not have to go around beating on their chests and publicly announcing their virtue. When they do exist in police departments they are in a minority and on a continuum of officers would appear on the extreme left (see below).

Continuum of Officers in Corrupt Departments

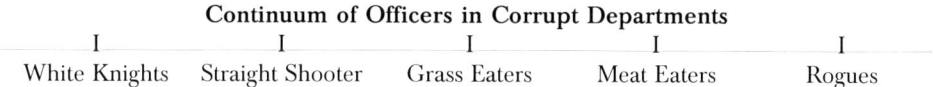

White Knights   Straight Shooter   Grass Eaters   Meat Eaters   Rogues

2. STRAIGHT SHOOTERS. These are "honest" officers who will overlook the indiscretions of other officers. They do so for pragmatic reasons (don't make waves, there is nothing one person can do, I'm not going to be a snitch, etc.) or for reasons of comradeship (we have to protect each other; cops don't turn in other cops). Not being comfortable with turning in a fellow officer, these officers will accept the fact that other officers engage in some patterns of corruption and misconduct, but not others. As one officer related to me, "I never took a bribe and I always refuse gratuities, except for free coffee, for which I always leave a big tip. However, if someone gets their head thumped, not 'LA style,' but a police rap to get their attention, I didn't see it." Officers in

this category in a corrupt police department generally suffer in silence or seek out corruption-free assignments.

3. GRASS EATERS. As stated previously, these officers engage in some corrupt activities as the occasion and opportunity arises. However, most will have their limits and engage primarily in accepting gratuities, occasional kickbacks, and opportunistic thefts.

4. MEAT EATERS. These officers actively seek out opportunities for corruption. They come to work with the idea of making money. They will develop the corruption potential of their beats and assignments.

5. ROGUES. The rogue police officer is one who is thoroughly corrupt and considered an aberration even by the **meat eaters**. The rogue will often commit highly visible shakedowns of citizens, felony fixes, and even direct criminal activities. Fortunately, they are a minority even in the most corrupt police organizations. New Orleans Police Officer Len Davis, currently on Louisiana's death row for setting up a hit on a woman who filed a brutality complaint against him, is the consensus prototype of a **rogue** police officer. In addition to the murder he orchestrated, Davis created a police-officer drug protection gang. A Harlan County, Kentucky deputy sheriff and drug trafficker pleaded guilty to the facilitating the murder of a man running for sheriff in 2002 (WLEX TV, 2009). He was afraid that if the man won the election he would fire him. On the continuum, officers such as Davis and the Kentucky deputy sheriff, are on the extreme right and in small numbers, i.e., rotten apples.

Included within the **Rogue** category are those few officers who were criminals or members of gangs who join police departments and continue their criminal behavior on the job. New York City Police Officer Emmanuel Perez is alleged to have been a member of a violent gang that robbed drug dealers in Manhattan, Queens, and Philadelphia before he joined the NYPD (Fisher & Weiss, 2010). It is alleged that he continued to be a part of the gang for the eight years he was an officer, supplying the gang with NYPD raid jackets, fake Miranda cards, bulletproof vests, badges, and guns. Allegedly, he participated in over 100 robberies that netted over $2 million.

Generally speaking, corruption in corrupt police organizations is uncovered through a scandal. Actions on the part of both **white knights** and **rogue officers** have led to scandals. A **white knight** blowing the whistle to the media or an external agency, or the outrageous behavior of a rogue cop cannot be covered up. The investigation and prosecution of police officers in corrupt police departments is usually handled by an outside agency.

CORRUPTION CONTROL

Obviously, the first step in corruption control is to recognize the possible patterns (Chapter 8) and the corrupt practices that can take place in the organization. The administrator must also recognize that police corruption can never be entirely eliminated from any police organization. That is an unrealistic expectation. Just as a society without crime will never exist, a police organization where no corruption occurs will never exist. As we have explained, the police occupation is a Morally Dangerous Occupation and will always be so. Some members of the occupation will succumb to the temptations. However, corruption can be controlled and managed by a three-pronged effort directed toward (1) decreasing the opportunity, (2) undermining group support for corruption, and (3) increasing the risk.

Decreasing the Opportunity

Stance of the Administrator

The police chief executive must convey his posture on corruption to the department and the public. This is especially true for those administrators who have been hired as change agents after a public scandal. If corruption has been a problem in the past, the new CEO must recognize that he/she has the duty to inform the officers that the practices will end. The reform administrator must convey to all potential applicants that only the honest should apply. Former FBI Director Louis Freeh said that all agents must adhere to what he called a "Bright Line Policy" – lying, cheating, stealing, sexual harassment, and alcohol or drug abuse would not be tolerated. Of course, the new reform executive is not in the position to grant general amnesty for past events, especially those that involved serious criminal violations. However, the new law enforcement executive officer can set the tone for the agency by developing an anticorruption policy with its attendant rules and procedures. The department's policy will set the limits for all members of the organization.

A Note on Policy Development

Policy is defined as the principles and values which guide the performance of a departmental activity. These principles and values are "attitude forming" in the sense that they tell departmental personnel how to think about performing their duties (Hoy, 1982: 301). A policy is *not* a statement of what must be done in a particular situation. It is a statement of guiding principles, which should be followed in order to attain some departmental goal or objective. Policy should always be thought of as the framework for drafting procedures and rules and regulations.

EXAMPLE
CORRUPTION
IACP

1. Purpose

The purpose of this policy is to prevent corruption from occurring in this law enforcement agency and to prescribe actions to be taken in the event that corruption is alleged and/or identified.

2. Policy

It is the policy of this law enforcement agency to establish proactive procedures to prevent corruption and to investigate and prosecute corruption to the full extent of the law, and administrative authority, when reported or identified (IACP Model Policy, 1989).

As one can see from the example, policy can be very broad and allow some flexibility and is subject to varying interpretations. Therefore, the agency must define the terms and limit the flexibility and discretion through procedures, rules, and regulations.

Procedures are the methods of performing an operation or the manner in which the task is to be performed. Procedures are different from policy in that they direct the action to be taken within policy guidelines. Policy and procedures are both objective oriented; however, policy establishes limits of action while procedures direct responses within these limits (Carter & Dearth, 1984). Procedures allow for some flexibility within limits and they are usually found in instructional materials and manuals as well as in policy statements. Accompanying procedures are rules and regulations.

EXAMPLE (IACP)
CORRUPTION PREVENTION IV.

Procedures

2. Code of Ethics

This department will maintain, periodically review and update a Code of Ethics. Each new employee will be required to read and place his/her signature at the bottom of a copy of the Code of Ethics as an indicator that he/she has read and understands the standards of conduct set forth in the Code of Ethics.

3. Rules of Conduct (ROC)

The Rules of Conduct shall appear in front of the policy manual to emphasize their significance. New employees will be instructed in the ROC. The ROC will be reviewed annually for relevance, timeliness, adequacy and completeness.

Rules and **regulations** are actually synonymous and refer to specific requirements or prohibitions, which prevent deviations from policies or procedures. A violation or a rule/regulation usually invites disciplinary action. If policies are "attitude forming" and guide judgments, rules are "behavior forming" and govern behavior. Rules are restrictive and allow for no flexibility or discretionary behavior. They should only be used when absolutely necessary to insure compliance with some desired behavior or action. Unfortunately, some police administrators confuse rules with policy and procedures and believe the only way to control behavior is through a proliferation of rules and regulations. This is self-defeating because the proliferation of rules and regulations creates an illusion of control yet not genuine control. This simple solution ignores the purpose of policy development and the effects of training, education, and good supervision. Even though too many rules may be counterproductive, there are instances where police behavior or misbehavior must be prevented. For example: **Rule** – All confidential informants and drug buys will conform to control, bookkeeping, and accountability procedures.

EXAMPLE (IACP)
CORRUPTION PREVENTION

Narcotics and/or Drug Enforcement:
   a) Two or more officers must be present to affect any arrests resulting from a planned drug operation.

b) All confidential informants and drug buys will conform to control, bookkeeping, and accountability procedures.

c) All evidence will be processed strictly according to the policies and procedures governing the property and evidence functions.

In addition to writing realistic and meaningful policies, procedures, and rules, the law enforcement executive must also ensure that his or her public statements on the subject of corruption are not unrealistic and pompous. Telling the press and the troops that "Police officers in my department arrest everyone who breaks the law. There will be no opportunities for corruption," "Corruption starts with a free cup of coffee," "There will be no fat cops eating apples in this department," will be viewed with skepticism and disgust. Police behavior should be guided and directed by realistic expectations. If you don't mean it don't say it.

It should go without saying that the law enforcement executive's behavior should conform to his/her public pronouncements and the department's policies, procedures, and rules. However, this is not always the case. There have been several recent well-publicized examples where the attitude has been "do as I say, not as I do." A chief accepting free rooms and meals, even though out of his home city, because of his/her position raises ethical issues and invites criticism.

Educating the Public

As part of his/her efforts to decrease the opportunities for corruption, the chief executive officer must educate the public concerning their efforts in corruption control. He/she may have to make public appearances before civic and professional groups where restaurant owners, barkeepers, construction firms, etc. are present and explain the department's policy on gifts and other gratuities. At first he/she may face some opposition and the "comment that it is my business and I will do what I want." However, once they understand that it is department policy for its officers not to accept the offered gifts and gratuities, things should straighten themselves out. They should be informed of the risk they are creating for the officer should he/she accept the gift or gratuity. They should also be encouraged to report any solicitations by police officers.

Increased Supervision

In today's world, police officers, often totally alone and unobserved, may be placed in a position where the money from a bribe or drug shakedown opportunity may be more than an entire year's salary. Corruption thrives best in poorly run organizations where lines of authority are vague and supervision is minimal (Goldstein, 1975: 42). Increased supervision can somewhat eliminate the opportunity for this to happen. Increased supervision means more than putting more sergeants or lieutenants on the shifts or in the precincts.

Additional supervision means giving police managers the authority and responsibility for anticorruption efforts. Supervisors must understand that they have the primary responsibility for identifying, eliminating, and controlling corruption. They should be trained in the techniques, investigative approaches and procedures to carry out their responsibilities. Top and middle managers must be held strictly accountable for corruption that occurs in their areas of responsibility.

Sustained Action and Monitoring of Legal and Illegal Corruption Hazards

The story is often told of sociologists spending enormous amounts of money researching for vice activities where $100 to an experienced cab driver would get the same information. Sometimes we wonder why police administrators at the top and middle management could not identify corrupt activities in their commands. There are certain activities and businesses that are natural corruption hazards and indicators of possible police citizen collusion. These must be closely monitored to decrease the opportunity for corruption. In 1979, Ward and McCormack in *An Anti-Corruption Manual for Administrators in Law Enforcement* listed numerous corruption hazards and indicators. Their list is still valuable today. A partial listing follows:

BARS, GRILLS, CABARETS AND BOTTLE CLUBS

Hazard

The acceptance of money gifts, free food and drinks by members of the department from owners and operators of bars and grills, cabarets and bottle clubs to overlook violations of the Alcoholic Beverage Control Law, the Health Code, Traffic Regulations and Administrative Code.

Indicators of the Problem

Unexplained visits by department members to bars, grills, cabarets, and other licensed and unlicensed premises, indicated by:
- failure to notify the radio dispatcher of visit
- failure to notify supervisor on patrol
- No arrests, summonses, or other police action taken when necessary, and failure to make proper reports.
- Improper or incomplete investigations of crimes occurring on or near premises.
- a specific pattern of visits to the premises members on and off duty.
- The presence of illegal parking in the vicinity without proper police action being taken.

Numerous complaints from the public alleging:
- disorderly premises
- overcharging for meals, drinks and services
- adulterated liquor and wine
- Credit cards lost or stolen from clothing checked in cloak rooms or from individuals on the premises.
- Police cashing personal checks that subsequently are returned to the bank due to insufficient funds.
- Assaults on patrons by employees or persons on the premises.
- Improper or no police action taken when police are summoned with complaint to premises for cause.
- Taxicab drivers, hotel employees, and others bringing people to pre-arranged specific locations like bars, clubs and hotels for a fee.
- Unlicensed premises (bottle clubs) selling alcoholic beverages. Premises frequented by persons who are obviously narcotic addicts or prostitutes. Without appropriate police action subsequently taken, individuals being injured in the vicinity of licensed premises under circumstances that might indicate that the injury occurred within the premises.
- Receipt of written or verbal communications alleging an improper presence of police in the premises or alleging some police corruption.
- Business being conducted during prohibited hours.
- Through personal observations, premises are frequented by known gamblers or racketeers without intelligence reports having been received from patrol service units.

Follow-up inspections reveal that complaints, referred to other commands for action, are not being acted upon effectively.

Inspection of records reveals that cases resulting in arrests or summonses have an inordinately low conviction rate for some premises.

Procedures for Control

Routine visits prohibited. Inspections should be conducted on a directed basis by the precinct commanding officer.

Commanding officer or executive officer should direct superior officers to make frequent observations of suspected premises and persons suspected of corrupt practices.

Information received from within the department and the public should be verified.

Conduct personal interview of complainants, when deemed necessary. Personally inspect and analyze department records to detect possible trends or patterns of police action in connection with premises under suspicion.

Carefully observe members of the department suspected of having a drinking problem that would cause them to become amenable to corruptive efforts by others.

CONSTRUCTION SITES

Hazard

The acceptance or solicitation of money, gifts and building materials by police to overlook violations of the law pertaining to the regulation of construction.

Indicators of Problem

- unexplained visits to construction sites by police while on and off duty.
- police observed placing building materials into department vehicles or into their private vehicles.
- identifiable violations which create safety hazards for pedestrians or which impede traffic flow at construction sites apparently being overlooked by police.
- written or verbal complaints received from the public alleging violations at construction sites without proper police action being taken.
- complaints received from construction workers or site managers alleging excessive enforcement.
- unusual summons activity by a member of the department, followed by sudden inactivity.

Procedures for Control

Direct written or verbal communications to site managers informing them of departmental policy and requesting their cooperation in enforcement. Advise them that the offer of a gratuity to a public officer is a crime and that the person making the offer is subject to arrest. Superior officers should make frequent observations of sites to insure adequate enforcement of pertinent laws and to observe the conduct of police observed at construction sites without sufficient reason for their presence.

Carefully examine summons and other records to detect signs of pressuring site managers by department managers.

Inspect construction sites immediately upon receipt of complaints.

HOTELS AND RESTAURANTS

Hazards

The acceptance of free meals, free rooms, and Christmas gratuities from owners and operators of hotels and restaurants to overlook parking, health codes, administrative code violations and laws pertaining to public morals.

Police unofficially assisting owners and operators of these premises in maintaining order.

Indicators of Problem

- Unexplained visits to the premises by police on duty and off duty.
- Receipt of written or oral complaints alleging members are obtaining free meals and rooms.
- Observations of violations of laws inside and in the vicinity of the hotels and restaurants without adequate enforcement activity for correction.
- Complaints from the public alleging violations of the liquor laws and the laws pertaining to gambling and prostitution that should have been discovered and reported by members of the department.
- Complaints, especially those alleging improper police action, of assaults on the public by employees of hotels and restaurants.
- Hotels and restaurants having a known policy of free meals, rooms, etc., for "man on post."

Procedures for Control

Make independent observations of premises for an evaluation of any crime problems that may exist.

Direct observations to detect the furnishing of unwarranted police service.

Carefully examine reports on injured individuals and complaint reports, the origins of which may have been in a hotel or restaurant instead of the location where actually reported taking place.

Compare the findings revealed by observations of suspected premises with arrest reports and with the results of other completed investigations.

Disseminate current departmental policy to members and to the owners, managers, and employees of hotels and restaurants and request their cooperation. They should be advised that an offer of a gratuity is a crime and that the person making the offer is subject to arrest.

Provide adequate sleeping facilities in the station house for police who need these facilities.

PARKING LOTS

Hazard

The acceptance by police of money, gifts, free parking privileges, and Christmas gratuities from the owners and operators of parking lots to overlook violations pertaining to their businesses.

Indicators of Problem

- Violations of traffic regulations and congested, vehicular traffic in the vicinity of the entrances to parking lots.
- Parking of customers' automobiles on streets in violation of departmental regulations.
- Deliberate inattention to violations by members on patrol.
- Unexplained visits to the parking lots by police while on and off duty.
- Written or verbal communications received alleging that police frequently observed overlooking violations.
- Complaints from parking lot owners and employees that they are unnecessarily receiving summonses for borderline violations.

Procedures for Control

Observe and inspect patrol supervisors to observe that laws concerning parking lots are being enforced fairly.

Inspect daily activity reports to detect unusual and suspicious trends of activity.

Frequent observations of persons and places susceptible to corruption efforts.

REPAIR SHOPS, GARAGES, TRUCKING COMPANIES

Hazard

The acceptance by police of money, gifts, and free services from owners and operators of repair shops, garages, trucking companies, and vehicle rental companies to overlook violations of the law pertaining to traffic regulations and to general business laws.

Indicators of Problem

- Double parking and parking on sidewalks in the vicinity of said businesses, without proper police action being taken.

- Loading or unloading in no loading zones resulting in the obstruction of sidewalks.
- Streets or sidewalks being used as storage areas.
- Major repairs, other than emergency repairs being performed in the streets.
- Receipt of numerous complaints about noise of trucks and cars, without any corrective action taken by patrol service units.
- Written and oral communications received from the public alleging collusion between members of the command and the business.
- Unexplained visits by members of the command on or off duty to the businesses.
- An inordinate number of rented automobiles recovered through arrests or recovered as abandoned, by specific members of the command. Arrest records could indicate a desire for rewards from the companies.
- Complaints received from operators and owners of the businesses, alleging excessive harassment by members of the command.

Procedures for Control

Direct superior officers to observe and inspect businesses frequently to ascertain that traffic regulations and general business laws are being properly enforced. Inspect departmental records to discern possible trends like a lack of summons activity.

GYPSY OR UNLICENSED CABS

Hazard

The acceptance or solicitation by police of money and gifts from gypsy cab drivers and operators of livery car services to overlook violations of traffic regulations.

Indicators of Problem

- Stopping an inordinate number of gypsy cabs without arrests being made, summonses being served, or adequate reporting made by members of the command.
- The receipt of a number of written or verbal communications from gypsy cab operators alleging harassment by members of the command.
- Rumors circulating within the command concerning the acceptance of bribes from gypsy cab operators, especially if they are related to specific members of the command.
- Unexplained visits by police on and off duty to gypsy cab offices or garages.

- Failure by patrol services to take corrective action concerning traffic conditions and unnecessary noise in the vicinity of gypsy cab offices and garages.

Procedures for Control

Direct superior officers to observe and to supervise closely members of the command in the enforcement of regulations governing gypsy cabs.

TRAFFIC VIOLATIONS

Hazards

The acceptance or solicitation by police of money and gifts to overlook traffic violations.

Indicators of Problem

- Excessive stopping of motorists by police without comparable summons or arrest activity.
- serious traffic and safety conditions-illegal parking, street repairing of automobiles, sidewalk parking, and low enforcement activity — left uncorrected by department members.
- Written and verbal complaints received from the public alleging no enforcement of traffic regulations or alleging payment to police for special treatment.
- Receipt of complaints alleging police officers attempted to extort money to overlook violations.

Procedures for Control

Direct superior officers to observe places and persons in areas of traffic to insure adequate enforcement and to prevent corruptive practices. Closely supervise members assigned to traffic control or parking enforcement duties.

Frequently inspect activity reports to discover possible corruptive practices.

TOW TRUCKS

Hazard

The acceptance or solicitation of money, gifts, and free services by members of the department to overlook violations of the laws governing tow trucks and to compensate police for referring operators of vehicles in accidents to specific companies.

Indicators of Problem

- An inordinate percentage of towing business being handled by a very few towing companies.

- Tow truck operators violating traffic regulations without corrective action being taken by patrol officers.
- Verbal or written complaints, received from the public alleging collusion between members of the command and tow truck operators.
- Members of the command observed in possession of business cards of towing or body-and-fender repair companies.
- The receipt of a substantial number of written and verbal communications from tow truck operators alleging harassment by members of command.

Procedures for Control

Superior officers on patrol should respond to the scene of all accidents requiring tow service.

Direct superior officers to frequently observe suspicious towing operations and suspected department members.

Initiate follow-up investigations of selected collisions involving a tow to determine any possible police corruption.

Distribute to motorists at accident scenes handout sheets describing laws pertaining to tows.

PROSTITUTION

Hazard

The acceptance and solicitation of money and favors by police from prostitutes to overlook violations of the laws relating to prostitution and prostitution-related offenses.

Indicators of Problem

- Unnecessary familiarity with known prostitutes while on and off duty.
- Failure of the uniformed patrol service to adequately control public nuisance conditions when prostitutes or pimps congregate on streets to actively solicit patrons or when hotels, massage parlors, bars, and apartments are apparently being used by prostitutes.
- The presence, on or off duty, of a member of the command not on police business, at locations frequented by known prostitutes.
- Recurring arrests of the same prostitutes as a harassment technique by individual officers for reasons other than impartial law enforcement.
- Written and verbal complaints from the public alleging collusion between members of the command and prostitutes.

Procedures for Control

Observe frequently suspicious areas of prostitution, pimps, prostitutes, and police to determine if any corruption patterns exist.

Initiate follow-up inspections to determine what action has been taken by plainclothes units regarding information supplied to them by patrol officers.

GAMBLING

Hazard

The acceptance of solicitation of money and gifts by members of the department from individuals involved in illegal gambling activities to overlook violations of laws regulating gambling.

Indicators of Problem

- Known gambling locations operating within the confines of the precinct without proper intelligence reports being submitted by members of the command.
- crowded parking conditions in the vicinity of suspected premises, especially during evening hours, that indicate possible organized card or dice games.
- Large numbers of people entering a business establishment like a candy store, shoe shine parlor, or grocery store and leaving without having made a purchase.
- Numerous observations of known gamblers at specific locations.
- Members of the command, while on or off duty, in the company of known gamblers or frequenting locations suspected of gambling activity.
- Failure by patrol officers to correct public nuisance relating to gambling.
- The receipt of written and oral communications alleging that members of the command are permitting gambling to take place.

Procedures for Control

Initiate frequent observations of individuals, locations, and members of the command suspected of being involved in corruption relating to gambling.

Direct superior officers to observe suspicious gambling locations frequently. Initiate follow-up inspections by the commanding officer to determine whether intelligence reports are being submitted for all suspected locations and persons within the command.

NARCOTICS

Hazard

- Prior to booking, the unlawful release of prisoners in exchange for money, narcotics, or other gifts.

- Unwarranted dismissal of court cases after police conspiracy with offenders.
- The withholding of contraband by police for private use, future sale, or the practice commonly known as "flaking" or placing evidence of a crime on a person who does not actually possess it.

Indicators of Problem

- An arrest pattern by specific officers which indicates a concentration of arrests for loitering and narcotics trafficking by people waiting to buy or sell.
- Repeated observations of police at locations frequented by narcotics users, especially when no other police business is occurring at those locations.
- Despite the receipt of complaints, narcotic locations flourishing without proper police action being taken.
- A pattern of complaints by prisoners alleging that money, other valuables, and narcotics are missing after the suspects have been searched by police.
- A pattern of complaints that charge improper search and seizure.
- A pattern of allegations of evidence being placed on a supposedly innocent person to justify an arrest.
- An unusual number of court cases being dismissed because of incomplete or faulty court affidavits, poor testimony, or non-appearance of specific members of the department.
- Members of the department spending money presumably in excess of their income.
- Possible narcotics use by members indicated, in addition to the usual physical signs, by excessive requests for emergency leave; excessive sick report time (noting type of illness), neglect of personal appearance; constant fatigue; inadequate attention to duty; allegations or rumors of an individual's involvement with usage; unexplained disappearance from station house of property from personal lockers, vouchered property, and office equipment; and observation of a department member's associates.

Procedures for Control

Closely supervise subordinates in the field to insure the proper handling of arrests and searches.

Establish strict procedures for searches and the recording of evidence. Immediate search in presence of station house supervisor and recording of evidence should be made. Supervisor should issue a receipt for evidence that the arresting officer can place in his memo book.

Hold frequent conferences with superior officers and community groups to obtain information related to suspected practices in narcotics enforcement.
Initiate frequent independent or parallel observations of narcotic locations and of suspected officers.
Frequently review individual records to determine suspicious trends in arrests, dispositions, and investigative results.
Train members in current departmental procedures and policies.
Hold periodic, unannounced locker inspections to discover the unlawful withholding of evidence or contraband.
Superior officer review all narcotic arrests, especially those that are dismissed in court.

As stated above, the examples used were from a draft of a manual developed by the New York City Police Department (McCormack & Ward, 1979: 27). This does not mean that smaller departments cannot use them. They give an idea of what to look for and how to possibly control the incidence of these behaviors. Obviously, the larger the department and the community where the department is located will influence the opportunities for corruption and misconduct.

Undermining Group Support

Every occupational group socializes new members into the group. These occupational groups can create informal rules concerning deviant (rule breaking) behavior. The social isolation of the American law enforcement community and their withdrawal into their own group for support – group solidarity – creates a situation whereby the law enforcement officer becomes subject to intense peer group pressure. This peer group can supply the rationalizations for corrupt acts. Some of the more common rationalizations are: law enforcement is a low-paying job, these are just fringe benefits or perks of the job, it is covered by insurance, these people like the police, they are respectable people, it is "clean money," everybody does it, if you don't do it nobody will trust you, he is a criminal and it is illegal money, etc. The end result can be that the new officer is provided with a list of "safe" or tolerated patterns of corruption and misconduct.

What we can have in a law enforcement agency is a situation whereby the deviant officer (engaging in corruption or misconduct) is encouraged by the protection of his peers and the group's deviant set of values. The group can also isolate and ostracize those who do not support the deviant values. Fortunately, the same group that can support deviant values can be channeled to support nondeviant values (more on this later).

Increasing the Risk

If the peer group can be enlisted in the control of corruption, this will increase the risk for the deviant officer. If the officer contemplating an act of corruption or misconduct understands that he or she will not receive support or tolerance from his/her peers, this is often enough to deter the act. This is a positive approach. Unfortunately, some negative actions must be taken even when the peer group supports nondeviant values.

Internal Policing

Obviously, not every agency is large enough to have a separate unit for internal affairs. However, someone must be responsible for internal policing in every police department regardless of size. The Internal Policing policy must be based on two concepts. The first is that all complaints against officers, especially those involving serious misconduct or corruption, should be handled and investigated with the same tenacity and techniques as would be used against any suspected violator. The agency does not want to be criticized as having one set of rules for officer's accused of misconduct and crimes and another when citizens are involved. The second basic concept is that the investigation should not stop even if the officer resigns. The matter must be resolved. The officer who chooses to resign may be guilty of a crime and may need prosecution. This will also prevent the practice common in some states whereby officers who resign under investigation are hired by other agencies.

Proactive or Reactive Internal Policing

A decision must be made whether or not the agency is to pursue a proactive or reactive policy of corruption control or even a combination of both approaches. Reactive control is confined to the investigation of complaints from citizens, victims, officers, and other outside sources, etc. Obviously, complaints would also be investigated in a proactive approach. However, in a proactive approach the internal policing unit would seek out corrupt officers and check on corruption-producing conditions.

There are disadvantages to both approaches. In a strictly reactive policy, the actual likelihood of risk of discovery is very low. The police bureaucracy often presents a significant obstacle for anyone wishing to register a complaint against an officer. A strictly reactive policy usually leads to the conclusion that any corrupt officers identified are rotten apples.

There are also several disadvantages to a proactive policy. For one, the "headhunters" charged with investigating fellow officers may one day be their partners or superiors. Several agencies, in an attempt to deal with this, make a tour in Internal Affairs mandatory for all midlevel managers. This may be a good solution because officers assigned to investigating other officers for long periods of time sometimes cease to be fair and objective investigators. Others have dealt with this problem by making it a mandatory assignment for promotion from sergeant to lieutenant.

Another disadvantage of the proactive approach is that it does not take long to create a sense of paranoia in the agency. Police organizations because of the myriad number of rules and regulations are often punishment-oriented bureaucracies. If a very active proactive Internal Affairs unit is added to this punishment-oriented atmosphere, paranoia runs rampant. Most of the studies on police stress have found that the majority of the police stress comes from the agency. It may be just as bad on the individual officer to work in a corrupt organization as to work in an organization whose goal is 100 percent corruption and misconduct free and works hard at accomplishing that goal, primarily through proactive Internal Affairs. Nevertheless, unless an outside agency is used to investigate corruption and misconduct, the agency must use some proactive strategies to increase the risk of corruption.

Proactive Strategies

EARLY WARNING SYSTEM. The IACP in a 1989 publication produced for the Department of Justice, *Building Integrity and Reducing Drug Corruption in Police Departments*, suggested an Early Warning System to identify potential problem officers, integrity breakdowns, and management weaknesses. They recommend that data be gathered in at least four categories: officer complaints, assignment, shift or tour, and report types. Although complaints on officers will be collected, the system is not unduly focused on the individual officer because it examines the assignment and shift for a possible explanation of the complaint. For example, some assignments, regardless of the officer may receive certain types of complaints. Officers working vice may receive numerous entrapment complaints as well as officers working drug units may receive an inordinate number of excessive force complaints. That certainly does not mean if the same officers working these assignments keep receiving complaints that there is not a problem.

The Early Warning System would routinely gather data from the following reports: (1) any discharge of a firearm whether accidental or duty-related; (2) excessive use of force reports; (3) any motor vehicle damage; (4) any loss of equipment; (5) injured on duty reports; (6) use of sick leave in excess of five days, or a regular pattern of using one or two sick leave days over long periods; and (7) all complaints, including supervisory reprimands and other disciplinary actions. I would also add all reports on resisting arrests and assaulting an officer. These are very good reports to identify violent men or officers needing additional training.

The authors of the report were quick to point out that any of the seven reports by themselves do not imply corruption or misconduct, but they could point out a trend or indication of a problem. For example, extended sick leaves and injuries are not incidents of misconduct, but they may point out an officer in need of medical, psychological, or social intervention. We will return again to Early Warning systems again in Chapter 11 when we discuss ways to control all unethical police behavior.

UNDERCOVER POLICE OFFICERS. Officers known for their honesty or rookie officers can be recruited to act as the eyes and ears of the internal policing unit. Obviously, when this practice becomes known, it is going to raise the paranoia level of the organization. I would suggest that it only be used in those departments with a history of corruption and an entrenched "Code of Silence."

SOLICITATION OF ANONYMOUS COMPLAINTS FROM OFFICERS. Anonymous complaints from citizens or officers can be very useful in a proactive strategy against corruption. However, they should be treat-ed with objectivity and fairness to the officer identified in the complaint. They are not to be assumed to be true. Nevertheless, anonymous complaints from officers provide a vehicle whereby an officer can identify a deviant coworker without suffering any ill effects from the peer group.

CORRUPTION PATROLS. A substantial part of the proactive Internal Affairs unit should be spent in patrolling and monitoring possible corruption locations. Known "shot" houses, gambling locations, areas where prostitution is know to occur, bars, and the other potential indicators of a problem identified earlier must be monitored.

Interviews of Arrestees and Individual Who Work in Corruption Assignments

The Internal Affairs Unit should conduct random interviews with arrestees and individuals who work in high corruption assignments such as vice and narcotics.

"TURNAROUNDS." A tactic that is usually abhorrent to most police officers is the use of turnarounds. That is, granting immunity to corrupt officers for testimony against other officers or using them as undercover agents. The department using turnarounds can expect damaging publicity as soon as their use is made public. This tactic should only be used as a last ditch effort against entrenched corruption where the Code Of Silence is pronounced. However, turnarounds and undercover officers can greatly reduce the incidence of corruption if judiciously used. We will return to this topic in Chapter 11.

INTEGRITY TESTS. Another tactic that brings on adverse publicity from both within and without the police organization is the use of integrity tests. This means creating artificial situations to give police officers the opportunity to commit crimes. Obviously, this tactic should also be used judiciously and sparingly.

Examples of integrity tests that have been used are:

1. Students or officers posing as drunks to see if money could be stolen by police officers or jail officials.
2. Wallets containing money or other valuables turned over to officers for safekeeping and return to owners.
3. Planting money or other valuables in illegally parked or abandoned vehicles.

4. Routing packages of supposed narcotics to officers who were led to believe the narcotics are real.
5. Sting Operations. Setting up businesses as fronts; pornographic shops, illegal gambling and drinking establishments, legal establishments operating illegally, to see if police officers will accept payoffs.
6. Sting operations when officer illegal activities are suspected.

Slayton, Texas police officials suspected that one of their officers was using marijuana and stealing evidence so they set up a sting to catch him. He was dispatched to collect a lost purse left on the bleachers of a high school. The purse contained cosmetics, two ounces of marijuana, and two $100 bills. The officer turned in the marijuana but kept the money (Carver, 2010).

The FBI in an investigation of thefts by police officers in the Milwaukee area planted more than $17,000 in a vacant store and set up hidden video cameras. Milwaukee police officer and a state agent from the Division of Criminal Investigation, who was also a former Milwaukee police officer (28) years were sent to search the store. The state agent was charged with the theft of $1,000 (Vielment, 2010).

Rogue New Orleans Police Officer Len Davis, mentioned earlier, was discovered during a FBI sting operation when a confidential informant reported his illegal activities. He was videotaped and caught on wiretaps engaging in corrupt practices with undercover federal agents. Davis was actually caught on tape ordering the murder that landed him on death row and celebrating when he learned of the murder.

Chapter 10

ABUSE OF AUTHORITY

INTRODUCTION

Police abuse of authority is "any action by a police officer without regard to motive, intent or malice that tends to injure, insult, trespass upon human dignity, manifest feelings of inferiority, and/or violates an inherent legal right of a member of the police constituency in the course of performing 'police work'" (Barker & Carter, 1994: 7). There are three forms of abuse of authority. First is physical abuse, which incorporates brutality and police violence: that is, the officer's use of more than necessary force to effect an arrest or search and/or the wanton use of any force under the color of the officer's authority. Second is psychological abuse, which occurs when an officer verbally assaults, harasses, or ridicules a citizen. The third type of abuse, legal abuse, occurs when police officers violate a citizen's constitutional, federal, or state's rights. Included within this type is convicting the innocent, an especially egregious form of legal abuse. Legal abuse will be discussed under Noble Cause Injustice.

The first two forms of abuse of authority, physical and psychological abuse, can occur in any police-citizen encounter. However, they are most likely to occur in proactive police-citizen encounters because of aggressive police tactics. The effect of the professional model (reform model) of policing to control corruption and inefficiency resulted in the crime-fighter image, which increased the abuse of authority (Brown, 1981: 288). The professional model's primary objective was crime fighting. The professional model's principle method of crime fighting was/is aggressive patrol. The primary tactic of aggressive proactive patrol was/is the field stop. The result of field stops often was, and is, abuse of power and citizen resentment. A field stop is an exercise in pure power, and nobody likes to feel powerless (Rubinstein, 1973: 233). In most criminal cases, the result comes about without outside control. In most citizen-police encounters, there is no review or control by the judiciary, supervisors, or the department. This in itself increases the likelihood of physical and psychological control.

USE OF FORCE

As stated earlier, the use, or potential use of force is at the core of the police role. The police have it within their power to use any number of instruments/techniques that can lead to injury or death: handcuffs, batons and nightsticks, flashlights, knives, stun and TASER guns, physical techniques (choke-holds, hog-tying), tear gases and pepper sprays, dogs, vehicles, etc. Any of these instruments/techniques can and have been used excessively and when not warranted. The unreasonable and unnecessary use of force is our focus.

During an arrest, force may occur in four situations. The officer/s may have to use force to effect or complete the arrest. The subject may not actually resist, but he or she may not willingly cooperate either. In the event that the subject resists the arrest, the officer or officers may have to use force to overcome that resistance. On occasion, the officer/s may have to use physical force to maintain the subject in custody or to regain custody should the subject attempt to escape. Lastly, officers may legally use force up to and including deadly force to defend themselves or others.

Unreasonable and unnecessary use of force includes wanton or intentional use of physical force by a police officer. Any wanton or intentional use of force used during an arrest situation or while the subject is in custody for the purpose of punishment is unreasonable and unnecessary and therefore, by definition, an act of police brutality. A U.S. Border Patrol Officer pleaded guilty for assaulting a Mexican national who was in custody (DOJ, June 3, 2010). The officer admitted that he kicked the victim, struck him in the stomach with a baton, and threw him to the ground without any legitimate law enforcement reason to use force. The victim was assaulted in custody and in the processing center. This incident demonstrates that not all use of unnecessary force occur during arrests but when the victim is in custody and in a police-controlled setting.

There are several possible reasons why an officer might engage in an act of brutality. He or she may be the pathological personality who enjoys physically abusing or hurting others. Many experienced police officers have probably come into contact with such individuals in their careers. These violent individuals are a small minority of the police occupation. Police departments are well advised to keep good records on resisting and assaulting arrests along with records of shooting incidents. Violent individuals are soon identified through proactive efforts and should be dealt with as soon as possible. A good psychological evaluation at the initial screening process can usually eliminate most of these individuals.

Some instances of unnecessary force are the result of fear, with the officer overreacting to what are, or what the officer perceives to be a dangerous situation. Some officers reacting to cultures or individuals whom they do not understand may believe that physical force is an absolute necessity in the "street jungle." This will be compounded in those departments that hire from the majority and place them in minority settings.

Verbal abuse and provocation by the victim often leads to unnecessary use of force. Officers provoked into using unnecessary force must understand that their actions will be examined later in a calm environment. An Oklahoma Highway Patrol Officer was recorded on two dashboard cameras kicking a handcuffed intoxicated and verbally abusive female two or three times after she spat on him (Baker & Kelley, 2010). The officer claimed he was defending himself and reacted on instinct. The officer pleaded no contest to a misdemeanor assault and battery charge and resigned from the department. Other officers on the scene were prepared to testify that the officer used unnecessary force in responding to the spitting. Two Lincoln, Alabama officers were sentenced to 22 years in prison for beating to death a man who cursed at them (APg, 2009; Hendon, 2010). The first officer pulled the victim out of his car and hit him in the head with a flashlight, knocking him to his hands and knees. The second officer, a sergeant, kicked him in the side. The first officer then continued to beat and kick the prostrate victim. The sergeant on appeal told the judge that he merely shoved the victim, not kicked him. The judge ruled that because of his rank the sergeant was guilty by omission for not restraining the other officer.

Three Baltimore police officers were convicted in federal court of civil rights and obstruction of justice charges for the physical abuse of a 17-year-old arrestee (U.S. Department of Justice, 2010). The teenager and an officer got into a verbal argument and the officer took off his badge and gun and challenged the teen to a fight. When the teen turned down the challenge, the officer pepper sprayed him. Later when the two of them were alone, the officer struck the handcuffed teen in the face with his baton breaking his orbital bone and fracturing his jaw in two places. The officer turned in a false and misleading report to cover up the assault. A second officer admitted that he lied to the FBI and also assaulted the teen. The third officer, a sergeant, admitted that he engaged in obstruction of justice to cover up the assaults. These two officers testified against the first officer after their pleas.

Demonstrators have often tried and successfully provoked officers into using force. In the age of the camcorder, officers have to be aware that film footage of police using unnecessary and unreasonable force can help any cause or group. Dealing with dissent is extremely difficult in free societies, and presents challenges to the police. Nevertheless, a police officer does not have the legal right to strike an individual who has insulted them or called him/her a profane name, but sometimes the officer may be pushed beyond endurance. Actually, an officer who reacts to such abuse and provocation has compounded his or her problems because now they will have to lie to a supervisor, on a report, or even in court to escape disciplinary action.

The May 2007 Immigrants Rights May Day demonstration in Los Angeles was broadcast nationally and internationally. There were disturbing images of riot-clad officers from the LAPD Metro Unit firing rubber bullets into a crowd of women and children and roughing up reporters. Then LAPD Chief William Bratton issued an apology and the Department's report was self-critical and concluded that the top commanders did not adequately plan for crowd control, failed to train officers, and that many officers did not know who was in charge (Anon g., 2008). The report also stated that when things spiraled out of control, no supervisor or command staff intervened. The commander in charge was demoted, his second of command was reassigned, and 17 officers and two sergeants were recommended for discipline.

Unnecessary force is also used against certain groups and individuals as punishment. Many officers believe that physical force is acceptable under certain circumstance: for Contempt of Cop, to command respect, to obtain information, or to punish certain classes of offenders (sex offenders, child molesters, hardened criminals). Often classes of individuals, such as gang bangers, bikers, radicals, hillbillies, "assholes," "skels," dirt bags, etc., are likely to become victims of brutality.

Those who resist arrest or run from the police in a vehicle pursuit are particularly vulnerable targets of police use of force. My research – and experience – into police pursuits has led to the conclusion that most injuries to the fleeing driver, and sometimes the occupants, occurs when the pursuit has ended and the parties are in custody. Every police officer who has been on the job for over a year knows this, even though police executives are still reacting with surprise when these "tune-ups" and "thumpings" are caught on tape. These injuries occur, for the most part, because the officer/s are still pumped up with adrenaline and mad. They take their revenge. Resisting arrest incidents are particularly likely to end up with the excessive use of force. Numerous officers through the years have told the author that any force short of killing the suspect is acceptable whenever an individual resists an arrest.

> When someone resists arrest you have to teach them a lesson. He may kill the next cop who tries to arrest him. My sergeant says there is no resisting unless the man goes to the hospital. So we send them [resisters] to the hospital.

Exact information on the police use of force is not known; however, there have been efforts to obtain the data. Section 210402 of the 1994 Violent Crime Control and Law Enforcement Act requires the U.S. Attorney General to gather data and make an annual report to Congress on the use of excessive force by police. The second annual report estimated that 0.2 percent of the population over the age of 12 had been "hit, held, pushed, choked, threatened with a flashlight, restrained by a police dog, threatened or actually sprayed with chemical or pepper spray, threatened with a gun, or experienced some other form of force" in 1996 (Greenfield et al., 1997: iv). The report concluded that the use of force is rare in police-citizen contacts and is usually provoked. However, police use of force against certain minority groups in some U.S. cities may be a problem, according to the report.

One author, writing just after the Rodney King incident, stated that African Americans, Latinos, and other minority males in Los Angeles are singled out by the Los Angeles Police Department and the Los Angeles Sheriffs Department for "special attention, physical abuse, brutality, and sometimes death" (Hoffman, 1993: 1471). Hoffman attributes this abuse to the patterns and practices of the two departments' use of military tactics in the War on Drugs, gangs, and crime. Both departments are well known for their hard-nosed, aggressive crime-fighter style of policing.

Many civil rights groups, such as the American Civil Liberties Union (ACLU), the National Association for the Advancement of Colored People, and Amnesty International, have complained that the present aggressive police strategies and zero-tolerance policing have led to increased use of force. Whether or not such complaints are true is a matter of controversy. However, the ACLU reports that since police departments have instituted restrictive policies on the use of deadly force, the number of incidents has dropped – as much as 35 to 40 percent in the 50 largest cities (ACLU, 1997: 15). This drop has been accompanied by a drop in the racial disparity in the use of deadly force. However, most of this drop might be a direct result of the 1985 U.S. Supreme Court's decision in *Tennessee v. Garner*. This landmark decision limited the use of deadly force to only those instances where the suspect posed a threat of serious injury or death to the public or the police officer. Prior to this decision in some states, deadly force could be and was used to prevent the escape of all felony suspects.

The crime-fighter model with its aggressive police tactics is alive and well in American policing, particularly in the War on Drugs, specialized paramilitary units, zero tolerance, and quality of life policing (see below). According to some, the war mentality, with its emphasis on crime fighting and preoccupation with the coercive use of force, has licensed the use of force in many police organizations (Kleing, 1996: 96).

The crime-fighter image also predominates among the police in Great Britain, even though crime fighting is a minor part of their work duties (Holdaway, 1984). The use of force against citizens occurs in Great Britain for the same reasons as in America: when police authority is challenged, when officers are assaulted, when danger is present, and as punishment, such as at the end of police chases (Holdaway, 1984). The constables' working rules allow for force under these circumstances. It is summary justice. "Just dessert" are adjudicated and administered by Hilton's [English city] officer (Holdaway, 1984: 130).

The Civil Rights Division of the Department of Justice in recent years has vigorously prosecuted the unnecessary use of force. Numerous police officers and correctional officers have received prison sentences for civil rights violations. Individual police departments have also begun to take action. Two Youngstown, Ohio officers were fired for an assault on a paraplegic (Anon, k., 2010). One was fired for the assault and the other for not being truthful during the internal affairs investigation. An example of federal and local cooperation on instances of excessive force occurred recently in Tennessee. A Shelby County, Tennessee deputy was sentenced to 18 months in prison after pleading guilty to hitting a citizen in the head while conducting an investigation. The **Tarnished Blue Task Force**, a multiagency task force led by the FBI and staffed with investigators from the FBI, Shelby County Sheriff's Office, and the Memphis PD conducted the investigation. This same task force has sent several area police officers to prison for civil rights violations and corrupt activities.

NOBLE CAUSE INJUSTICE

We have made frequent references to Noble Cause Injustice throughout the book; now we will provide a more thorough discussion of this perennial problem of policing – the Morally Dangerous Occupation. The first presidential commission to examine the American Criminal Justice System, the 1931 Wickersham Commission, devoted two of its 14 volumes to the unlawful enforcement of the law by American police officers. The reformer, Ernest Jerome Hopkins, in one of those volumes, said that American police operated under what he called the "War Theory of Crime Control" and used unlawful means, primarily third-degree interrogation techniques to control crime (Hopkins, 1972: 314–47). Hopkins pointed out that the police, after using the third-degree techniques, had to perjure themselves to conceal their unlawful acts and sway the court. The police frequently perjured themselves to obtain convictions. All the police actions were justified by the phrase "This is war." Hopkins summed up the philosophy:

> This criminal is the enemy: he is to be defeated by being quelled. Being the enemy, he has no rights worthy of the name. He is to be met by the weapons of war. Individual rights, including those of noncombatants in wartime, are subject to evasion like the rights of noncombatants in wartime. The policeman is a peacetime soldier. If the bullets go astray, if civil rights are suspended, those are accidents in warfare that is waged in crowded cities. (Hopkins, 1972: 319)

Nevertheless, the Wickersham Commission declared, "The fight against lawless men, if waged by forbidden means, is degraded almost to the level of a struggle between two lawbreaking gangs" (Hopkins, 1972: 13). Hopkins and the Wickersham Commission were railing against Noble Cause Injustice.

Noble Cause Injustice involves the idea "Yes, I did something wrong, but justice demanded it, not tolerated it but demanded it, because I could put the guy away who otherwise wouldn't be successfully prosecuted" (Moore, 1997: 63). Heffernan, in his *Typology of Disinterested Rules Violations*, identifies two types related to what he calls noble cause misconduct: (1) meting out justice via violations of the Constitution and (2) promotion of social order via violations of the Constitution (Heffernan, 1985: 7–8). Heffernan opines that the first type occurs because officers, through illegal searches and arrests, seek to punish those systematically involved in crime that are believed to be relatively immune from prosecution. Known criminals are getting their due. The second type occurs because officers believe that the courts do not understand the value of preventive police actions. According to many officers, restrictive concepts such as probable cause and articulable suspicion unfairly handcuff the police in maintaining public order.

Feeling that one is right to do what one does is not always the right thing to do. Nevertheless, Brown (1985: 285) stated that a good pinch even at the expense of legality was an occupational norm for the police he studied. Herbert (1997: 52) reports that the "creative use of probable cause" in the Los Angeles police in their "pooping and snooping" activities (field stops) was encouraged and praised by the department.

If the officer's behavior is discovered, the state will suffer via the exclusionary rule; however, in most instances, nothing happens to the officer administratively or in the courts. There is the possibility of discovery, but the probability is low. Nevertheless, if it is discovered or raised, the officer will have to lie. Once engaged in lying, perjury under oath is a possibility. Whatever the rationale, lying by police officers under these circumstances is an especially egregious violation in a free society with the traditions of liberty and openness, governmental accountability, and fear of central authority (Marx, 1958: 94). Heffernan states that if an officer feels that the aims of criminal justice are being subverted by the current rules of his office, the officer has two choices: (1) resign or (2) protest the rules while still honoring them (Heffernan, 1985: 14). Nevertheless, documented incidents have occurred.

In an incident reported to the Florida Criminal Justice Standards and Training Commission (certifies and decertifies Florida police officers) in 1995, a Metro-Dade police officer lied on a police report and again in sworn testimony (www.sun-sentinel.com/news/copd2b.htm). The officer said she saw the suspect drop a bag of cocaine. Another police officer and witnesses contradicted this. She said that she arrested the suspect in his car, also contradicted, and found a pistol under the driver's seat. Testimony revealed that another police officer found the pistol in the trunk. The officer, instead of being terminated, received a 20-day suspension. In Florida, decertification is automatic for felony convictions or misdemeanor involving perjury. In addition, for 45 crimes ranging from stalking to engaging in sex on duty, officers can receive penalties ranging from probation to revocation.

According to Holdaway (1984), British police officers sometimes "construct or adjust the evidence" in court to ensure a conviction. They adjust, refine, and correct evidence to render the suspect's guilt more obvious. However, not all British officers – as with American officers – engage in this behavior.

> Two of Hilton's officers had arrested subjects for attempting to take a motor vehicle. Their colleagues discussed the arresting officers' unwillingness to construct the evidence in order to gain a conviction: "And it is a foreign [another police subdivision] court anyway, so there we are. You see, he doesn't believe in that sort of thing." (Holdaway, 1984: 74)

Holdaway reports that procedural rules are often considered irrelevant by the British police as they go about their daily duties. The occupational culture of the British police condones the use of "verbals" or "working the oracle." A verbal is an oral statement of admission or incrimination invented by the arresting officer or interviewing officer and attributed to the suspect (Holdaway, 1984: 109). They, like their American counterparts, feel that they have privileged information knowing that the suspect is guilty and that the officer only helps the evidence along.

> [Police Constable] When you have a legal system that allows people to get off and makes you break the law to get convictions, then you have to be slightly bent. (Holdaway, 1984: 113)
> [Police Constable] . . . It's part [verbals] of being a policemen. If you know their guilty, there's nothing wrong, and if you're not willing to do it, you shouldn't be in the job. (Holdaway, 1984: 113)

Noble Cause Injustice in the War on Drugs

The result of the 30-year War on Drugs has been an unwinnable war by police officers wearing black masks, dressed in fatigues with buzz haircuts, and trained in the use of submachine guns, explosives, and chemical weapons. These police "ninjas" are the street warriors in the ultimate "us against them" mentality (see Kraska, 1996).

The current War on Drugs is not this country's first drug war. August Vollmer, writing in 1936, stated:

> The deteriorating effects of drugs upon the victims, and the intimate associations of the drug habit with the commission of crimes, are so inescapably evident that the police are encouraged to employ every means known to them to eliminate the supply agent and the peddler. (Vollmer, 1971: 108)

Vollmer also said that drug addiction is not a police problem and not to be solved by policemen. He said it was first and last a medical problem that could only be solved by "scientific and trained medical experts" (Vollmer, 1971: 118).

The noted police historian James Richardson (1974: 103) pointed out that the police cannot serve the dual purposes of enforcing the drug laws and observing the constitutional protections of individual rights. He states that full enforcement of the drug laws would be possible only in a police state "where the police would be allowed to stop and search at will and where there could be no question of police infringement of constitutional guarantees since there would be no guarantees" (Richardson, 1974: 103). Richardson stated that if society asks the police to serve both purposes, they would be tempted to bypass the legal structure. They have done this, resulting in many instances of Noble Cause Injustice.

The popular anticrime-punish-the-criminal rhetoric leads many citizens to agree with the police that the guilty, particularly drug offenders, deserve less than strict constitutional protection. There is public support for the officers who violate civil rights and lie to make a case stick against the dirt bags. Witness the popularity of the television show *NYPD Blue*, where constitutional violations of the guilty – as determined by the detectives – especially Andy Sippowitz – was an art form. However, the police in a democracy are the guardians of our civil liberties. The "avenging angel syndrome" to which some officers fall prey can be very dangerous to the officers and the citizens.

Carter states that the officers he studied rationalized their actions as "perhaps a form of 'winning' or 'revenge'" (1990: 90). Examples of this winning or revenge behavior included:

- False statements to obtain arrest or search warrants against known drug dealers/traffickers
- Perjury during hearings and trails of drug dealers.
- Planting or creating evidence against known drug dealers.
- Overt and intentional entrapment.
- Falsely spreading rumors that a dealer is a police informant, thus placing that person's safety in jeopardy.

In Jacksonville, Florida, two members of the sheriff's department's elite anticrime unit, including the sergeant in charge, were arrested for falsifying an incident report to justify an illegal entry into an suspected drug house (News4Jax.com; Schhoettler, 2010). The officers were executing what is known as a "knock and talk" technique – officers knock on the door of a suspected drug house and see if they can get consent to search or smell dope smoke or see drug or drug paraphernalia when the door is opened. No one was home and the sergeant in charge took an air-conditioning unit out of a window and directed the officers to climb in the window. The house was searched and no drugs were found. The sergeant then directed an officer to file a burglary report justifying their entry. Two members of the anticrime unit reported the sergeant to the department's Integrity Unit. The officer who filed the false report pleaded guilty to filing the report at the behest of his sergeant and agreed to testify against him. The investigation has led to additional charges against the sergeant for beating a suspect with a police handheld radio and ordering his unit to kick down a door when they did not have a search warrant.

The undersheriff is quoted as saying "Sometimes what happens is these guys go out there and they think they're doing a good deed, and they forget that we have rules. . . . And by God, that's what makes us who we are, is the rule of law. . . ." Disturbing also is that the 14-year veteran sergeant had 12 citizen complaints and had been sent to counseling three times. Should he have been identified as a problem officer earlier?

In 2009, four Oakland, California police officers were fired for falsifying sworn affidavits used in illegal drug raids. They told the judge issuing the search warrants that they had field tested drugs when they had not. In the aftermath of this revelation, 16 defendants had their cases dropped or dismissed.

Lies in Support of Perceived Legitimate Goals

The lies told to affect an act of Noble Cause Injustice are told to achieve some perceived legitimate goal, usually to put criminals in jail, prevent crimes, and perform other policing responsibilities. They are told because the law enforcement officer feels that his/her unique experiences in dealing with criminals and the public allow them to intuitively know the guilt or innocence of those they arrest or come into contact with. They feel this way independently of any legal standard. The officer/s convinced that the suspect is factually guilty of the offense may believe that the necessary elements of legal guilt may be missing, e.g., no probable cause for a stop, no **Miranda** warning, not enough narcotics for a felony offense, etc. Therefore, the officer feels that he or she must supply the missing elements to prevent a guilty person from walking. One officer told me during a training session that it was often necessary to "fluff up the evidence" to get a search warrant or insure a conviction. The officer will attest to facts, statements, or evidence, which never occurred or occurred in a different fashion. Obviously, when he/she does this under oath, perjury has been committed.

Once, a matter of record, the perjury must continue for the officer to avoid facing disciplinary action or even criminal prosecution. Whether or not this occurred in the O. J. Simpson trial is still a matter of debate. However, the evidence is overwhelming that at least one officer lied in that case. The Simpson trial introduced a new term into the discussion of police testimony – **testilying**.

Evidence of testilying did not first appear in the Simpson trial. In 1989, charges were dropped in a case against a cop killer and three Boston police officers were suspended with pay pending a perjury investigation. The perjury involved a Boston detective who "invented" an informant. The detective maintained that the informant gave the critical information, which was cited in the affidavit for a search warrant (*New York Times*, 1989: K9). The "no knock" search warrant's execution led to the death of a Boston detective. In 1991, the Boston detective who invented the informant was sentenced to five years probation for perjury (*Law Enforcement News*, June 15/30, 1991: 2).

One source critical of police testimony opines that testilying occurs because (Haas, 2006):

- Officers commit perjury to serve what they perceive to be "legitimate" law enforcement ends.
- In the viewpoint of most police officers, regardless of the legality of the arrest, the defendant is in fact guilty and ought to be arrested.
- When prosecutors are preparing for a trial, they often arrange "dry runs" as part of the trial preparation procedure. Frequently, prosecutors skirt along the edge of coercing or leading the witness
- As a result, impressionable young cops learn to tailor their testimony (commit perjury) to the requirements of the law.

The 1994 Mollen Commission investigating police corruption in New York City found that felony perjury in drug enforcement occurs:

- When officers unlawfully stop and search a vehicle because they believe there are drugs in it, officers will falsely claim in police reports and under oath that the car ran a red light or committed some other traffic violation.
- Once pulled over, the police officer will search the occupants of the vehicle as well as the vehicle – with or without consent – although the police officer will always indicate that they had consent.
- If consent is adamantly opposed by the occupants, the police officer will report under oath, that the contraband was in plain view.
- To conceal an unlawful search that does not involve a vehicle, police officers have been taught to report and testify that they saw a bulge in the person's pocket or saw drugs and money changing hands.
- To justify unlawfully entering a residence where officers believe drugs or cash can be found, cops commit felony perjury by claiming

that the had information from an unidentified civilian informant. (Haas, 2006)

In 2009, an international drug kingpin was acquitted of all charges when a Canadian judge found that two senior RCMP officers had lied to the court. The judge called the RCMP sergeant and corporal "liars" after finding that they made false statements to get wiretap authorizations and then lied in court to cover up the false swearing.

The officer who lies in these instances must employ creative writing skills on official reports to ensure that the written chronology of events is consistent with criminal proceedings, regardless of what actually happened. As I have often stated in police training sessions, the problem with lies is that the truth has instant recall; lies don't. If an officer tells a lie in a criminal case, he/she is going to have to constantly recall what was written on the official report, what was told to the sergeant, to Internal Affairs, and on the stand. Sooner or later it may all come unraveled.

Noble Cause Injustice can, and does, have tragic consequences. One, is the possibility that the innocent will be convicted of crimes they did not commit. When an instance of an innocent person being convicted is discovered, the police respond that this is a rare event. This is probably true, but what if the innocent is convicted because of the intentional misconduct of the police?

Convicting the Innocent

There have been several notorious cases in the United Kingdom where the innocent have been convicted by the overzealous actions of the police. The Guildford Four refers to a case in 1975 where four men were convicted of a pub bombing which killed five. They were in prison for 14 years before their convictions where overturned and three police officers were accused of fabricating evidence. Also in 1975, The Birmingham Six were convicted of two pub bombings that killed 21. Their convictions were overturned in 1991 and three police officers were charged with perjury. Both of these cases occurred during a period of IRA violence and there was intense pressure on the police to arrest the bombers. The perfect conditions for Noble Cause Injustice to occur existed in both of these cases – highly visible crimes receiving a lot of media coverage and intense pressure on the police to make arrests.

In one of the most egregious miscarriages of justice in British history, known as the "Cardiff Three," 34 people were arrested, including 15 retired police officers and five serving officers (Hodges, 2009). Thirteen of the 34 were charged, including nine retired and three serving officers. The officers' allegedly "moulded, manipulated and fabricated" evidence to secure a conviction of three men for the murder of a prostitute in 1988. One of those convicted in 1990 for the murder confessed and implicated the other two men. He was 26 but had the mental age of 11. The convictions were overturned on appeal in 1992 when the judge ruled that his 13-hour confession was "bullied and hectored" and a "travesty of an interview" (Bennetto, 2005). Three witnesses claimed that the police bullied them into making false statements. DNA analysis identified the real killer in 2003 and he was sentenced to life in prison. An inquiry was launched into the botched investigation, leading to the arrest and charging of the officers. There are examples of the same miscarriages of justice in the United States.

In 1986, Louis Eppolito, one of the two NYPD cops who became known as the Mafia Cops because they moonlighted as Mafia hit men for the Lucchese crime family, framed a postal worker, Barry Gibbs, for the murder of prostitute (Hays, 2010). The miscarriage of justice became known after Eppolito and his partner, former NYPD Detective Steven Caracappa, were convicted in 2006 of eight murders, kidnapping, and other crimes. The former postal worker served 19 years before he was released from prison. Prosecutors speculated that Eppolito framed Gibbs, who had a drug habit and knew the prostitute, to divert attention from mobsters who committed the murder.

The Director of Douglas County, Nebraska's crime lab and the county's chief crime scene investigator was accused of planting blood evidence in a 2006 murder investigation that lead to wrongful conviction of two men for murder (Funk, 2010). The police and he thought that the men were guilty. In fact, a tape shows that the police used improper interrogation techniques to induce a mildly, mentally challenged suspect to falsely confess to the murder (Anon i, 2010). The men spent several months in jail before they were cleared after the real killers were found. The CSI director was convicted of evidence tampering and sentenced to 20 months for evidence tampering and two police investigators are being sued.

We have previously discussed the undercover Texas racist gypsy cop who falsely arrested and convicted 47 victims (42 black males) in

Tulia, Texas. The Texas governor pardoned all those convicted after the appeal judge called the officer a liar, thief, and racist. A Chicago man who spent three years in jail before being acquitted of his neighbor's murder in 90 minutes sued the city and the three detectives who claimed that he confessed to them, although there was no evidence or taped or written confession (Eldeib, 2010). The civil jury found that the detectives who were under pressure to solve the case had made up the confession and they awarded the man $1.3 million.

A corrupt Bureau of Alcohol, Tobacco, Firearms and Explosives (ATF) special agent and a corrupt Tulsa, Oklahoma undercover officer fabricated a drug bust that resulted in the conviction of a Tulsa man and his daughter in 2008 (Crockett, 2010; Gillham, 2010; Gillham & Harper, 2009; Terrtebone, 2010). The officers believed the two were drug dealers but could not prove it. They gave three ounces of methamphetamine to a confidential informant and coached him to testify that he bought the drugs from the man and his daughter. The two victims were convicted and sentenced to five and one-half years and two concurrent 10-year sentences respectfully. Both were released and had their drug convictions dismissed after the informant admitted he lied. The ATF agent pleaded guilty to stealing money, planting drugs, and framing innocent people. As part of his plea agreement, the former agent will testify against the Tulsa officer and others involved. So far 11 cases have been dismissed, including one where a man served five years of a 22-year sentence (Fullbright, 2010).

The current FBI investigation of the Camden, New Jersey Police Department, mentioned earlier, involves numerous examples where the innocent were convicted or the "guilty" were illegally convicted. Thus far 185 criminal cases have been dropped or convictions vacated. The four officers charged thus far worked in a special operations division assigned to patrol high-crime drug trafficking areas. One officer pleaded guilty and admitted that he and the other officers charged subjects after planting evidence, threatened others with planted evidence unless they cooperated, conducted illegal searches without warrants or consent, stole drugs during these illegal searches and arrests, prepared false reports, and testified falsely in court to conceal their illegal actions.

The corrupt Camden cops added drugs to the amounts found on the subjects at least 20 times and paid cooperators and informants with drugs for information. In one case, they falsely stated that one subject who weighed 325 pounds and walked with a cane ran from them and dropped drugs in his flight (Ann o, 2010; Katz, 2010). In another case the officers searched a suspect and his house and found no drugs. However, they held him until officers showed up with about $4,000 in crack cocaine. The suspect pleaded guilty for a three-year sentence rather than risk up to 20 years with no chance of parole for ten years. His sentence was vacated. A 20-year-old college student pleaded guilty to possession of marijuana for probation after the officers planted marijuana on him rather than face more time at trial. The conviction forced him to drop out of college because he lost his financial aid. His conviction was vacated.

The worst case scenario occurs when an innocent person is killed or injured during an instance of noble cause injustice. That is what happened in Atlanta, Georgia on November 21, 2006. Ninety-two-year-old Kathyrn Johnston was killed during the execution of a no knock search warrant by three plainclothes Atlanta Police Depart-ment drug officers. The officers cut off her burglar bars and broke the front door down. As the officers entered, Ms. Johnston, most likely fearing a home invasion, fired over the officers heads. The officers fired back 39 times, hitting Johnston five or six times. An officer handcuffed the dying woman who was pronounced dead on the scene. Finding no drugs in the house, the officers planted three bags of marijuana in the house and called an informant and told him to say he had bought crack cocaine at the house earlier. In the affidavit to get the search warrant, the officers stated that the police informant had bought crack cocaine at the location and they had video surveillance of the location. A federal probe was opened and one officer ratted out the other officers. The police sergeant in charge of the unit pleaded guilty to charges surrounding the shooting and received an 18-month sentence. The three officers involved pleaded guilty to conspiracy to violate civil rights resulting in death and were sentenced to 10 years, six years and five years respectfully.

The investigation revealed the planting of drugs and lying to obtain search warrants by the Atlanta Police Department (Atlanta Citizen Review Board, 2010). The Atlanta Citizen Review Board (ACRB), formed after the Kathryn Johnston killing, stated that the FBI report revealed that the sergeant in charge, a 23-year veteran, knew and allowed officers to "trade" search warrants with one another. One would swear that he had witnessed events that he never actually saw.

The sergeant also allowed officers to falsely assert that unregistered informants were reliable. The ACRB concluded:

> His [supervising sergeant] participation and ratification of unconstitutional and criminal activity helped to form the culture which led officers down the continuum of ethical compromise. His misconduct was not isolated and, as a supervisor, his behavior had a greater impact on the culture of those who worked for him and the resultant sense of betrayal by those he victimized and by the community as a whole. (page 5)

There were also allegations that other Atlanta officers falsified information on numerous search warrant affidavits; padded vouchers; testified that they drove informants to buys when they did not; rarely, if ever, conducted pat-downs before informants made buys; used unregistered and unreliable informants; and commonly used "hand offs." A hand off is a police technique where one officer provides probable cause to another officer to use for a search warrant. The information may or not be true. The second officer includes the information in his or her affidavit, saying that he or she has firsthand knowledge of the incident, clearly a lie (ACRB, 2010). Officers explained that the "hands-off" practice was used in order for drug officers to meet their quota, known as the "nine and two" requirement – each officer had to make nine arrests and two search warrants each month to meet accepted standards of productivity.

Police executives all deny that police departments have quotas for tickets, arrests, and other police activities and faced with an obvious example, define them as performance measure, numeric goals, or some other vague name. However, the reasonable man and all current or former law enforcement officers know they are pure and simple quotas. The Birmingham News obtained a memo written by the acting Birmingham post commander saying that each trooper should make at least three DUI arrests by the end of the month and that those that those who failed to do so could lose their day-shift assignments and opportunities for overtime pay (Faulk, 2010). Highway patrol officials said that although the poorly worded memo sounded like a quota, troopers do not have quotas. The memo was merely an attempt to get the troopers to step up efforts to cut down on impaired drivers. Sounds like the disingenuous statements given by politicians when caught in an obvious lie or contradiction in what they say and what they do. At a time like that, you have to say something. As a police officer once told me when we were discussing police quotas, "They can bullshit the citizens, but they can't bullshit us."

Now, let's turn our attention back to the discussion of the tragedy that occurred in Atlanta. The ACRB originally faced the usual accusation that the death of Ms. Kathyrn Johnston was the result of misconduct committed by a few rogue cops or bad apples. The review board gave three insightful reasons to dismiss that characterization in this instance. They said:

> The "bad apple" defense is flawed in three respects. It does not comprehend the scale of the harm a handful of dishonest officers, acting with impunity, can do, nor does it convey the impact those few bad apples, if not removed will have on the barrel. This defense also allows the organization to ignore responsibility for the systemic, organizational and management weaknesses. (ACRB, 2010:2)

This provides a good segue into a discussion of how we control police unethical behavior.

Chapter 11

CONTROLLING POLICE UNETHICAL BEHAVIOR

In Chapter 9, we discussed specific ways to control police corruption. In this chapter, we examine several general mechanisms for controlling all forms of police unethical behavior – organizational rule violations, corruption, and abuse of authority. We begin with the ideal control system – self-control.

SELF-CONTROL

The ideal control system of ethical control is inner; however, the real-world control is external (Kleing, 1996: 217). Individuals have, or should have internal "moral compasses" that distinguish between right and wrong. This moral compass is the result of the socialization process that begins at birth. This socialization process continues on to the workplace where occupational socialization has an important impact on police ethical behavior.

The police occupation in an attempt to select individuals with good moral compasses and the necessary qualities for police work has traditionally tried to *screen out* candidates who possess evidence of bad qualities: arrest records, history of bad debts, drug use, violent behavior, untrustworthiness, and so on. At times, this has worked, only to be defeated by other police occupational practices (Barker, 1977).

The police occupation has not tried to *screen in* candidates who possess the good qualities for police work (Gaines & Kappeler, 1992). Part of the reason for this is that there is no general consensus outside the possession of common sense (whatever that is and it often does not seem to be common) of the good qualities for police work outside the absence of bad qualities. Research in the area could possibly lead to reliable predictors for ethical behavior. Experienced police officers can often recognize the differences between good and bad officers. Every police officer with at least five years experience in the same department can usually name officers known for their unethical behavior. British officers studied by Holdaway (himself a police sergeant) were well aware of their colleagues who used verbals, adjusted the evidence, or used excessive force.

However we might wish for inner-directed officers, it must be recognized that ethical conduct is assisted or made more difficult by situational factors that include the organizational structure and peer group culture.

PEER GROUP CONTROL

Within the police organization, there are three patterns of social interaction, two internal to the organization and one external: police to police, police to supervisors, and police to the public. The first pattern of social interaction, police to police, has been described as a subculture with dominant values, one of which – loyalty – breeds a code of silence protecting miscreant officers. The socialization process of the police (academy, FTO and peer group) also emphasizes danger, mutual assistance, and loyalty as core values (Crank, 1998). The peer group can, and will, reinforce ethical behavior or provide rationalizations for unethical behavior (Barker, 1977; Barker & Carter, 1994). The occupational culture of police organizations is where officers learn their working behavior and good and bad habits. The occupational culture also creates the Blue Wall of Silence. The most disturbing aspect of most visible examples of police misconduct to the public is not that there are bad cops but that often when these events occur, there are so many good cops standing by doing nothing and then seeing nothing when asked about it later. Police organizations are continually asking others to come forward and provide information on crimes they have witnessed or give up information on peers, relatives, and friends. However, these same members of the public know the police are notorious for not doing so when it comes to their own.

A black Boston police officer in plainclothes was almost beaten to death by a fellow officer in 1995; yet, the other officers present, including at least one black officer, protected his attackers and those who took no action (Lehr, 2009). A Boston officer was quoted in the book as saying, "The test of loyalty on [sic] police department is number one: Will you lie for me? And if you won't lie for me, will you at least be silent?"

However, there are indications that the Blue Wall of Silence may not be as solid as once thought. Joan Barker's (1999) 20-year ethnographic study of the occupational subculture of the LAPD led her to conclude that traditional solidarity is breaking down with the influx of new officers, particularly minorities and women. This is evidenced by a proliferation of complaints against their colleagues. Coulson (1993) cites five cases (Claremont, Massachusetts; Cochella, California; Fort Lauderdale, Florida; Erie, Pennsylvania; and Denton, Texas) of officers filing complaints against their colleagues. Three of the complaints involved the use of excessive force. Whistleblowers among the police, although rare, do exist and several instances have been cited in this book.

The Board of Inquiry into the LAPD scandal reports that in 1996, 1997, and 1998, there were 30 cases where LAPD personnel were the primary witnesses in charges of misconduct against other officers (LAPD, 2000). The charges ranged from excessive force to neglect of duty.

Traditionally, the Blue Wall of Silence breaks down when careers and pension benefits are mentioned. The wall literally crumbles when prison time is mentioned. Police officers, like most offenders, will blow the whistle under these circumstances. However, one must distinguish between police whistleblowers. There are two types of police whistleblowers: the informer (traitor among the participants) and the informant (in possession of knowledge). The New York City Police Department informers, such as Bob Leuci, William Phillips, and Michael Dowd, betrayed those who were involved in corrupt practices. The Atlanta police officer who ratted out his coconspirators in the death of Kathyrn Johnston fits into this category as do the others cited in numerous incidents of testifying for reduced sentences or other considerations. They are Blue Rats, cooperating in their best interests. The NYPD informants, such as Frank Serpico and Joe Tromboli, provided information on corrupt activities, not their accomplices. These officers were essentially "good guys" reporting corrupt practices. A sergeant with the Polk County, Georgia jail pleaded guilty to using excessive force on an inmate in a restraint chair after several of his fellow detention officers reported his behavior to the sheriff who in turn reported it to the FBI.

Shame attaches, as it should, to the status of informers, a participant who has flipped out of self-interest. Shame should not attach to the informant who has reported misconduct because of a sense of duty. There is a huge difference between the individuals who blow the whistle because of the interests of the organization and the occupation and the cop who flips because he is trying to save himself. Often, the deals made with the police informer are like the deal made with the Mafia hitman Sammy "The Bull" Gravano – "shaking hands with the devil." Patrolman William Phillips (Knapp Commission) was a rogue cop engaged in far more serious behaviors than those he flipped on (Schecter & Phillips, 1973).

The current *Law Enforcement Code of Ethics* makes no mention of what a police officer should do if he/she discovers the corrupt behavior of another officer (Wren, 1985: 26). It should be clear that the discovering officer is the good cop betrayed by a bad cop and not the other way around. Wren (1985: 10) suggests the following addition to the code:

> The [police department] should safeguard the public and itself against [police officers] deficient in moral character or professional competence. [Police officers] should observe all laws, uphold the dignity and honor of the profession and accept its self-imposed disciplines. They should expose without hesitation illegal or unethical conduct of a fellow member of the profession.

The Washington, D.C. Metropolitan Police Department has a general order (MPD General Order 201.260) requiring police officers to promptly report misconduct or any violation of MPD rules to a supervisor. However, testimony to the special committee investigating corruption revealed that this rarely happened, and if it did, the whistleblowers were retaliated against (www.dcwatch.com/police/981006b.htm#Chapter 3:4). The committee stated that there was a culture of retaliation in the MPD. Following the report of the special committee, the Council of the District of Columbia enacted the Whistleblower Reinforcement Act of 1998, D.C. Act 12-239, to strengthen already existing legislation protecting whistleblowers.

The problems faced by a police officer discovering the unethical behavior of a fellow officer are virtually the same for all occupational groups. Welfel (1997) aptly describes the difficulties encountered by her fellow psychologists under the same circumstances. Both groups (police and psychologists) face competing values (ethical conduct and peer group culture) in moral decision-making. Loyalty to colleagues is a desirable characteristic in both groups. The police occupation, however, clearly is more dangerous and often requires less time to reflect and deliberate about ethical decisions (Welfel, 1997). One can easily examine the literature on the difficulty that certain occupations (lawyers, physicians, clergy) have with members not disclosing or shielding fellow members.

A civil suit filed by a Vineland, New Jersey police officer in May 2010 reads like a déjà vu case of what New York City Police Officer Frank Serpico went through in the 1970s. The 10-year veteran alleges that his police supervisors tried to silence him as he attempted to report illegal drug-related activities of his fellow officers. The complaint alleges that the police chief and the mayor, a former police officer, were also involved in the efforts to silence him. The officer first reported his suspicions to his immediate supervisors who ignored them. Next, he reported the alleged illegal acts in writing to his lieutenant, who became visibly upset and berated him for putting the information in a written report. Later, his sergeant and lieutenant met with him and stressed the need for secrecy and promised to forward his information to internal affairs. Nothing happened and the officer went to the chief. Again, no investigation, but the whistleblower was demoted for "jumping command," removed from the narcotic division and sent back to the patrol division, prompting him to file the civil suit.

SUPERVISORY CONTROL

Supervisory control, combined with quality leadership and training, is the manner in which the police occupation provides the external moral compass for officers to make ethical judgments in line with the police occupation and the organization. Proactive management oversight, particularly at the mid-level (sergeants and lieutenants), is the organization's first line of defense against unethical police behavior.

The Mollen Commission cited ineffective field supervision and the fear of disclosing corruption because of its adverse effect on the supervisors as contributing factors to the scandal (Baer, 1995). Nevertheless, there is little chance that field supervision can keep all bad cops from doing bad things. The nature of police work – individual or pairs of officers working alone under little supervision – works against close field supervision. There are too many police officers and too few supervisors (Vicchio, 1997). The nature of police actions also works against close supervision. Reactive police work (calls for service) occurs primarily in private settings (homes) and proactive police work (officer initiated) occurs primarily in public places (usually public streets), unobserved by anyone but the citizens and the officers. At times, the supervisors can contribute to abuse. If the supervisor urges or demands that officers make arrests, "some of them will ignore the law and the truth to improve their performance" (Rubinstein, 1973: 58). Supervisors who impose quotas, such as what happened in Atlanta, increase the risks that officers will cut corners or bend the laws and rules to meet the quotas, performance measures, numeric goals, informal standards, agreed upon standards, or whatever they are labeled.

Field supervision is only one part of supervisory control: auditing the officers' behavior is also part of the supervisor's responsibility.

Included within these audits is closely monitoring the charges that are most often used in cover-up charges (resisting arrest, assaulting an officer, disorderly conduct, obstructing and interfering with an officer). Repeated findings of a small minority of officers being involved in multiple incidents of alleged ethical violations and civil actions has made Early Warning Audit Systems necessary.

EARLY WARNING AUDIT SYSTEMS

Two hundred and thirty Chicago police officers with repeated complaints against them accounted for over 46 percent of the $16 million in judgments against the city from 1991 to 1994 (Nelson, 1995). The Chicago Commission on Police Integrity, appointed after the latest corruption scandal in two precincts, recommended an Early Warning System to alert command when an officer may be involved in a pattern of misconduct (Commission on Police Integrity, 1997). The

Christopher Commission, convened after the King incident, found that 183 Los Angeles officers had four or more allegations of excessive force or improper tactics, 44 had six or more, and 16 had eight or more (Christopher, 1991). One officer had 16 allegations. The New Orleans police officer convicted in 1996 of having a woman killed for filing a complaint against him had been the recipient of 20 complaints between 1987 and 1992 (ACLU, 1997: 18). Most of the allegations involved brutality. The officer had previously been suspended for 51 days for hitting a woman in the head with a flashlight. The ACLU has advocated Early Warning systems to identify officers who have an inordinate number of physical force incidents.

The U.S. GAO, in its report to Congressman Rangel, recommended an Early Warning system to identify potential problem officers (U.S. Government Accounting Office, 1998: 5). The consent decree entered into by the Pittsburg Police Department with the U.S. Department of Justice includes an Early Warning System to identify problem officers (Vera, 1998: 16). Amnesty International reports that, in an April 16, 1999 speech, before a national summit on police brutality, Attorney General Janet Reno endorsed Early Warning Systems to identify officers who engage in misconduct (Amnesty International, 1999: 4).

In mid-1995, following the murder convictions of the officer mentioned above, New Orleans instituted an Early Warning System called the Professional Performance Enhancement Program (PPEP). Officers are picked for this program based on complaints, use of force, and shooting incidents. The officers receive additional training, supervision, or counseling (Human Rights Watch, 1998). Based on the current problems in New Orleans, this program doesn't appear to have been very successful. Portland, Oregon has a "command review" that acts as an Early Warning System. The system reviews officers who receive five complaints within a year, three in six months, or two of the same type in six months (Human Rights Watch, 1998).

The institution of these Early Warning audit systems should act as a problem-solving approach to ethical violations. However, the administration's handling of the data generated is important.

Technical assists such as dash cams and live stream videos to the dispatcher and head mounted cameras will assist in officer safety and supervisory control. The Carmel, New York Police Department is putting streaming video feeds that allow the dispatcher to view incidents from the communication center. The car's lights and siren activate the stream video system. The news stem will serve four police functions: (1) safety – dispatchers can monitor traffic stops; (2) evidence – assist prosecutors in criminal cases; (3) safety and investigations – assist the department with crimes in progress; (4) discipline and control – assist the department in civilian complaints and other misconduct. Head-mounted cameras are being used on an experimental basis in Cincinnati and San Jose. The cameras will record interactions with the public and are to be turned on each time officers talk with anyone. The cameras are extremely expensive at this time and that is a drawback. Many officers do not welcome these technical assists and recognize them as enhanced supervisory control. I asked a local police officer if his department had installed dash cams in their cars and he replied, "No, and I hope they never do?" I replied why would you say that; they can help in court. "They can hurt you in court and before IA also," he replied. The officer is right.

ADMINISTRATIVE REACTION

An indifferent attitude toward officer misconduct can quickly erode the confidence of the public and the police officers (Delattre, 1989). The organization must create an atmosphere that reinforces the good character and motivations of a carefully selected and trained workforce. The atmosphere must, to some extent, be punishment-oriented for those who commit unethical acts and be supportive of those who do not and who report the unethical behavior of others. A purely punishment-oriented approach is counterproductive but quite common in police organizations, especially those that are solely reactive in nature. Videotaping high-risk encounters (pursuits, booking, protests and disturbances, raids, warrant servings) can serve as an administrative check on use-of-force incidents; failing this, it could provide evidence for disciplinary actions. The new NYPD management tool Compstats is being used as an administrative weapon against police misconduct (Silverman, 1999: 187). Compstats involves the diagnosing, analyzing of crime and quality of life problems to discover their commonalities and patterns. The technique is also used to monitor and address civilian complaints of misconduct. Included within the analysis are FADO (force, abuse, discourtesy, and obscene language) citizen complaints citywide – by borough, precinct, and hour and time of day.

Often, the police organization does a poor job of investigating corruption/misconduct complaints when they come to its attention. The Mollen Commission investigating corruption in the NYPD reached this conclusion:

> The shock is not that there are corrupt officers but that too often police departments are incompetent when it comes to investigating corruption.
>
> Judge Milton Mollen

Judge Mollen said on a number of occasions that the NYPD was incompetent and inept in their dealing with corruption. Therefore, an administrative reaction must include a fair, timely, and competent investigation of all complaints.

GYPSY COPS

Police administrators, individually and as a group/association, must take action to stop gypsy cops. Gypsy cops are nomadic officers who have gotten in trouble in one department and are terminated without having their certification withdrawn or reported. Because they resign after a plea bargain, they can and do go on to work for another department. Gypsy cops are also a result of lax or nonexistent background checks. There are numerous examples of gypsy cops. A Dickson County Tennessee sheriff's deputy was fired in 2010 for waving a handgun around in a parking lot, while under the influence (Staff, 2010). He had been in the sheriff's department for two years after being fired from the Montgomery County, Tennessee Sheriff's Department after being charged with DUI and domestic harassment. He had been with Montgomery County for 18 years. A former St. Charles, Louisiana deputy sheriff who pleaded guilty to malfeasance in office in 1994 for shaking down Asian motorists was recently arrested for applying for another police position without revealing his arrest history (Hunter, 2010). The former deputy worked for two different agencies, one for seven years, before his arrest. The officer was given a five-year suspended sentence and served two years probation for his plea bargain and his record was expunged after the probation was completed. The corrupt officer who was convicted of a felony should have lost his certification.

There is no national system for certifying or decertifying police/peace officers. Instead, the police occupation relies on a chaotic and confusing system run by individual states. In 12 states – Alaska, Delaware, Georgia, Maryland, Missouri, Montana, New Hampshire, New Mexico, Oregon, Pennsylvania, South Dakota, and Tennessee – officers automatically lose their certification upon termination. Forty-three states have some system to decertify police officers who commit felonies or certain misdemeanors (www.pocis.net/policies.) Because of a complex mix of peace officers, especially elected officials and heads of departments, certain peace officers are excluded from decertification by the state certifying agency in most states: Arizona (elected sheriff); Colorado (Denver City and county sheriff deputies); Connecticut (state police, marshalls, and state attorney's inspectors); Florida (sheriffs and chiefs); Idaho (elected official, deputies serving civil processes, director of Idaho State Police, and parking or animal control officers); Illinois (state police and elected officials); Kentucky (sheriffs); Louisiana (chiefs and sheriffs); Maryland (heads and deputy heads of law enforcement agencies); Michigan (sheriffs); Mississippi (sheriffs, elected chiefs and constables); Montana (sheriffs); New Mexico (sheriffs); North Carolina (sheriffs); Ohio (State Highway Patrol troopers and chiefs of police); Oregon (reserve officers); Pennsylvania (state police, sheriffs and park rangers); South Carolina (sheriffs); Tennessee (state officers); West Virginia (heads of law enforcement agencies); Wisconsin (elected officials). The District of Columbia, Hawaii, Massachusetts, New Jersey, New York, Rhode Island and Vermont have a state agency for certification but do not have the authority to decertify.

The conviction on a felony or certain misdemeanor is a high threshold for decertification that leads to problems. West Virginia has such a standard and has only removed the certification of seven officers from the 2005–06 fiscal year (Harki, December 27, 2009). It has been called a "toothless process" that has resulted in numerous gypsy cops still holding certification in the state, including a West Virginia state trooper accused of raping women on duty in 2008 who became a police chief in a West Virginia city. A West Virginia county deputy sheriff resigned his job for firing his gun at his girlfriend's house; he is now a police officer in another city.

All terminations and any officer who resigns under investigation should be decertified or reported to a state clearing house as happens in Texas, although their reliance on convictions for revocation of certifications causes problems as we shall see later. Texas has had some horrendous incidents of misconduct by gypsy cops, including the national scandal in Tulia, Texas in 1999 (Blakeslee, 2005) where one racist gypsy cop, Tom Coleman, falsely arrested 47 defendants (42 black). The fact that the officer in one day in 1999 arrested 13 percent of the area's black adult population in a city of 5,000 population should have called for an investigation. Who were these drug dealers selling to, each other? The fact that no cocaine, what they were accused of selling, no cash, or firearms were recovered the day of the raids should have also raised a red flag. Instead, the defendants received a total of 750 years in prison and the Texas Attorney General named the rogue gypsy cop "Texas Lawman of the Year" for his outstanding narcotics work. There were other factors that should have caused suspicion about his "outstanding" narcotics work.

Undercover contract agent Tom Coleman hired with U.S. Department of Justice monies to fight the war on drugs in Rural America had little, if any drug experience and a flawed background check. The gypsy cop narcotic agent operated without using standard undercover techniques; he had no partner, no video or tape recording back-up, no fingerprint evidence, no notebook; notes were recorded on his leg, there was no supervision or debriefings. All convictions were based on his uncorroborated testimony. At the appeal trials, it was revealed that Tom Coleman had a checkered past with other police agencies that should have been easily discovered and disqualified him from the position in Tulia. Coleman previously worked for the Sheriff's Department in Cullman County, Texas where he walked out, literally in the middle of the night owing $7,000 in local bills and facing charges of stealing government property. The sheriff at Coleman's perjury trial said that he sent a note to the Texas Department on Law Enforcement Standards and Education stating, "It is my opinion that an officer should uphold the law. Mr. Coleman should not be in law enforcement if he is going to treat people the way he did [in] this town." There were also reports of at least one arrest and possible mental problems in Coleman's background. Evidence at trial revealed that Swisher County authorities, including the sheriff, knew that Coleman had been indicted for theft in Cochran County, Texas in 1997. Even after he was fired from Tulia, Coleman went on to work for three Narcotic Task Forces in 18 months until he was convicted of perjury in 2005. The judge conducting the defendant's appeals said that Coleman's testimony was "absolutely riddled with perjury" and that he was "the most devious, nonresponsive law enforcement witness this court has witnessed in 25 years on the bench in Texas (CBS News, July 4, 2004). Texas Governor Rick Perry pardoned all those convicted after learning that the judge accused Coleman of being a liar, thief, and racist.

In addition to the pardons issued by the governor, there were other reactions to this miscarriage of justice by the rogue gypsy cop. The Tulia defendants will share in a $6 million settlement of their civil suit. Texas passed the "The Tulia Law" requiring corroboration in undercover investigations. Texas now requires a form (F-5) to be sent to the Texas Commission on Law Enforcement Officer Standards and Education. All agencies before hiring an agency must call the Commission and ask for the F-5s from previous employers.

TEXAS COMMISSION ON LAW ENFORCEMENT OFFICER STANDARDS AND EDUCATION SEPARATION OF LICENSEE (F-5)

Honorably Discharged
-
-
-

General Discharge
__ Retired or resigned while under investigation for an administration violation and after the officer was advised in writing of the investigation
__ Retired or resigned while under investigation for a criminal(s) and after the officer was advised in writing of the investigation
__ Retired or resigned after receiving notification of pending disciplinary action, up to and including termination for an administrative violation
__ Failed to complete a field training program
__ Failed to complete agency probation period
__ Failed to complete required training under rule 217.11
__ Failed to complete TCLEOSE licensing requirements
__ Died while under investigation
__ Retired or resigned through mutual agreement with the governmental entity and agency __ is eligible __ is not eligible to reapply

Dishonorably Discharged

__ Retired or resigned in lieu of termination for a criminal offense(s) (**must attach an explanation of the criminal law being investigated**)
__ Terminated for a criminal offense(s) charges filed (**must attach contact information for court of record or district attorney's office**)
__ Terminated for a criminal offense (**no charges filed after review with the district attorney's office**)
__ Retired or resigned in lieu of termination for an admin. violation(s) of truthfulness or insubordination
__ Terminated for an administrative violation(s) of truthfulness or insubordination.

Adapted from Separation of Licensee F-5 5.5.2010
http://www.tcelose.state.tx.us

Unfortunately, lax, sloppy, or nonexistent background checks by police agencies can defeat any decertification system. The arrest of a Texas police chief, Michael Meissner, on seven felony charges, including possession or promotion of child pornography, promotion of prostitution, and engaging in organized crime points out problems with the Texas system (AP c, 09/16/2009). An equally nomadic cop, John Hoskins, brought the charges against Chief Meissner. Hoskins had been hired by 14 police agencies since 1999. There was bad blood between the two gypsy cops since that time (Nielsen, January 2, 2010). Meissners' charges were dropped in 2010.

The Texas system does not revoke certification without conviction, relying on the agency to make their employment decisions on thorough background checks and reasonable standards – in effect a "toothless process" perpetuating the gypsy cop problem. Any reasonable person, let alone a minimally qualified hiring authority police officer or government official should have questioned Meissner's employment history, 18 agencies in 20 years and four arrests. Reprimands were issued by the Texas Commission on Law Enforcement on two of these arrests, "tampering with a witness, a state jail felony" and "impersonating a peace officer, a felony, and operation of a security company without a license, a Class A misdemeanor," and not reporting them to the Texas Commission (Anon d, October 15, 2003). The cases were dismissed, but he was required to report them.

The employment history of the second gypsy cop, John Hoskins, should have raised enough questions to prevent his employment as a police officer.

Texas Commission on Law Enforcement
Officer Standards and Education
Personal Information

Michael C. Meissner   TCLEOSE ID
                                                           (P ID) 41822

Appointed As	Department	Service Time
Chief of Police	Little River Academy PD	0 years 7 months
Chief of Police	Hawley PD	0 years 1 month
Chief of Police	New Summerfield PD	0 years 0 months
Chief of Police	Caney City PD	0 years 8 months
Police Officer	Life School ISD	0 years 3 months
Police Officer	Bardwell PD	3 years 0 months
Police Officer	Lone Oak PD	0 years 1 months
Police Officer	Caddo Mills PD	0 years 3 months
Police Officer	Princeton PD	1 years 0 months
Police Officer	Methodist Medical CT. PD	0 years 9 months
Police Officer	Ladonia PD	1 years 5 months
Police Officer	Malakoof PD	0 years 10 months
Police Officer	Edgewood PD	0 years 10 months
Police Officer	Canton PD	0 years 2 months
Police Officer	Princeton PD	2 years 7 months
Police Officer	Crandall PD	1 years 2 months
Police Officer	Grand Saline PD	1 years 3 months
Jailer	Van Zandt Co SO	0 years 10 month

Public Record for WEBSITE accessed May 15, 2010

Texas Commission on Law Enforcement
Officer Standards and Education

John Hoskins

Department	Length of Service
Combine PD	6 months
Payne Springs PD	1 month
Wolfe City PD	14 days
Hawk Cove PD	3 months
Wolfe City PD	4 months
Wolfe City PD	4 months
Kaufman ISD PD	2 months
Saint Jo PD	5 months
Frankston PD	2 months

Emory PD	13 days
Ladonia PD	1 month
Bogata PD	4 months
Commerce PD	3 months
Bogata PD	3 months

Source: Nielsen, January 2, 2010

Why does "gypsy" exist? There are a variety of answers to this question ranging from sloppy, lazy, or nonexistent background investigations to systematic problems. The nomadic cop problem is aided and facilitated by the false sense of allegiance among many officers who do not report the transgressions of their fellow officers or are not willing to testify against them. The misconduct does not rise to the level of a criminal offense. Allegations are not backed by detailed investigations, either because the department does not have an internal affairs process, or the "stomach" to "wash their dirty linen" in public. They would rather pawn off a problem than deal with it.

Finally, many departments are desperate for experienced certified officers and take what they can get and hope for the best. The City of High Springs, Florida hired a highly experienced 13-year veteran police officer who had been terminated from the Sarasota County Sheriff's after being arrested for battery on two women when he was off-duty and drunk (Ryals, May 16, 2010). The officer's excuse was that he is an alcoholic who sometimes "blacks out" when drinking. One of the officers who recommend his hiring in spite of the termination is quoted as saying that "she can sympathize with him making a mistake while intoxicated." She goes on to say, "He is very, very qualified." "This young man is definitely SWAT team material." The Chief of Police was also impressed with the officer's qualifications and experience and said, "attracting someone of that caliber to High Springs would normally be very difficult." The chief also is quoted as saying that "he is surprised that [his] past has raised such a concern, especially because he [the chief] said other High Springs police officers have been hired in the past despite having less than perfect background checks." The new High Springs officer is currently suing his former agency for not helping with his alcoholism that he claims as a disability under the Americans with Disabilities Act as well as the Florida Civil Rights Act.

EXTERNAL ACCOUNTABILITY

All democratic police forces are subject to monitoring and accountability by outsiders (Bayley, 1997: 5). These outsiders include elected politicians; civil, criminal, and administrative courts; the media; and civilian complaint-review boards.

The Department of Justice's Civil Rights Division was created by Congress in 1957 and has had criminal enforcement powers over civil rights violations by police officers since its inception. Police officers, acting under color of law, can and have been prosecuted for civil rights violations, particularly for violations of excessive force and unwarranted seizures and false arrests. A new weapon has been added to their arsenal.

Since 1994, Congress has authorized the Civil Rights Division of the Department of Justice to bring pattern-or-practice civil suits for the declarative or injunctive relief against entire police departments instead of individual police officers. Congress passed this act as a reaction to the 1992 beating of Rodney King and the 1992 Los Angeles riots. The pattern or practice of behavior has to be conduct by police officers that deprives persons of rights, privileges, or immunities secured or protected by the Constitution of the United States (42 U.S.C. 1414). These pattern-or-practice suits can include excessive force, discriminatory stops, harassment, false arrests, coercive sexual conduct. and unlawful stops, searches, seizures, and arrests (Vera, 1998: 15). The violations include supervisory failures related to these behaviors. The Pittsburgh, Pennsylvania Police Department was the first to be sued under the pattern-or-practice concept. The police department entered into a consent decree that established comprehensive and specific measures to end systematic police misconduct.

Soon after the Pittsburgh case, the Civil Rights Division entered into a consent decree with the City of Steubenville, Ohio. Its police department was accused of engaging in a pattern or practice of excessive use of force; false arrests, charges, and reports; and improper stops, searches, and seizures. Steubenville police officers were alleged to have beaten witnesses of misconduct, falsified reports, and tampered with official police records in order to cover up misconduct (Vera, 1998: 16).

In April 1999, a report from the New Jersey Attorney General's Office concluded that New Jersey state troopers were engaging in racial profiling when stopping motorists for possible drug arrests. Amnesty International reports that the U.S. Department of Justice announced the same month that they had enough evidence of discriminatory treatment by the New Jersey state troopers to bring a pattern-or-practice suit (Amnesty International, 1999: 3).

Now, the Civil Rights Division of the Department of Justice can bring criminal prosecutions against officers, as in the Rodney King incident, or civil rights actions against entire police departments in pattern-or-practice suits as they have done in Buffalo, New York; Cincinnati, Ohio; Columbus, Ohio; Detroit, Michigan; Highland Park, Illinois; Los Angeles; Montgomery County, Maryland; Mount Pleasant, Illinois; and Washington, D.C.

EXTERNAL REVIEW BOARDS

Civilian review boards have been a contentious issue for the American police since first brought up in the 1950s. However, civilian review of police organizations in some form may be becoming the norm. According to the ACLU (1997), civilian review boards are the norm in 75 percent of the nation's largest cities. Eighty cities have them.

External review boards need not be confined to the traditionally understood civilian review boards. However, some outside entity should audit the police department's control of corruption and Early Warning Systems. The external board does not, and probably should not, control the investigation.

Chapter 12

CONCLUSIONS

The ethical violations discussed (rule violations, corruption, and abuse of authority) have existed in the police occupation since its inception in England. The various forms have continually surfaced in British and American police forces/departments throughout the short history of policing. Police reformers have always recognized that their work was a morally dangerous occupation. They recognized this in Codes of Conduct and numerous reform efforts. Nevertheless, the police occupational culture in many forces/departments has traditionally provided its members with ready-made rationalizations for many of these ethical violations (Ahern, 1972; Benton, 1977; Barker & Carter, 1994; Chevigny, 1969; Crank, 1998; Kappeler et al.; Manning, 1977; Skolnick, 1966; Rubinstein, 1973; Westley, 1970). Nevertheless, peer pressure, weakness in others, impulses, opportunity, and personal rationalizations (blaming the system, noble cause injustice) do not excuse lapses of character by the police (Kleing, 1996). Democratic societies have the right to expect ethical behavior among their police forces. Therefore, the occupation and the citizens of a free society must continue their efforts to control the ethical violations. The costs of police ethical violations are too great for the occupation and our free society to be ignored.

Police ethical violations inhibit the movement of the police occupation to a profession, reduce confidence in the police, violate the constitutional rights of citizens in a free society, victimize the innocent, imprison the innocent, and are costly. Suing the police is a popular and profitable venture for many attorneys. New York City has paid out $305 million over the last decade for claims of false arrest, wrongful conviction, and excessive force (Macdonald & Wilkinson, (2010). Between July 2006 and June 2009, Detroit paid out $19.1 million specifically for police misconduct allegations (Macdonald & Wilkinson, 2010). Detroit's total includes: $7.3 million for 18 people shot by police; $6.7 million for 50 suits for violations of constitutional rights; $2.4 million on two suits for wrongful deaths other than shootings; and $1.9 million on suits for assault and battery, false arrest, and imprisonment. Minneapolis paid out $885,622 for police misconduct incidents that occurred in 2007, $700,900 for incidents in 2008, and thus far $356,000 for 2009 incidents (McKinney, 2010). The City of Chicago paid more than $31 million in lawsuits involving Chicago police officers in 2009 (Martinez, M., 2009). Los Angeles has already paid out $13 million to settle suits arising out of the 2007 "May Day Melee." New York City paid a $9.9 million settlement to a man who served 19 years in prison for a crime he did not commit (Benoit, 2010). He was framed by the notorious NYPD Mafia Cops that were Mafia hitmen while on the job.

However, complicating the issue of suits against the police is the well-known practice of government entities settling them when it might be more costly to go to trial. The Township Council of Neptune, New Jersey paid $65,000 for an excessive force lawsuit even though their investigation found no wrongdoing on the part of the officers (Gladden, 2010). The mayor said settling the suit would save money. This kind of action has a devastating effect on officer morale and encourages frivolous suits.

There must be a two-pronged approach to controlling ethical violations: avoiding rotten apples and avoiding rotten structures (Delattre, 1989: 88). Avoiding rotten apples involves establishing higher standards for recruitment and selection and good educational programs for newcomers and experienced personnel. Rotten structures should be dealt with through a nontoleration policy by police leadership, institutional audit procedures to ensure accountability, systematic investigations of complaints and suspicious circumstances, and external review. There is a pressing need for a concerted effort to eliminate the structural causes of Noble Cause Injustice. The innocent should never be convicted or killed by overzealous or misguided police vigilantes who disregard the legal safeguards of a free and democratic society.

Any efforts to control the ethical violations of the American police are constrained by a lack of data on several issues. There is a need to have accurate information on the nature and extent of ethics training in American police agencies. The IACP, the world's oldest and largest police professional association, in their first and only attempt to learn this information from its members received a dismal 18 percent return on their survey (www.the iacp.org/pubinfo/Pubs/ethic.Train.htm). If the police establishment is not serious about the *Law Enforcement Code of Ethics* and ethical training for all officers (academy and in-service), then the code could be perceived as a compilation of useless homilies put forward by an occupational work group calling itself a profession (Barker, 1996). A 1993 Texas survey of training academies conducted under the auspices of the Law Enforcement Ethics Center of the Southwestern Law Enforcement Institute (response rate of 32.7 percent) revealed that an average of 6.73 hours of ethics training comprised only 1.6 percent of the total recruits' time (http://web2.airmail.net/slf/oct93/training.html). The study also found that ethics training was less than 1 percent of the total in-class time. The center has been training police ethics trainers since May of 1994.

Anecdotal evidence suggests that some departments that have experienced scandals are improving their ethics training. The Chicago Police Department's Education and Training Center instituted an ethics-training concept, Ethics Across the Curriculum, based on the ethics training used by the U.S. Naval Academy. Integrity issues will be part of the entire curriculum of the center (Commission on Police Integrity, 1997).

Following the Rampart Scandal, the LAPD began distributing the *Law Enforcement Code of Ethics* to every recruit class, directing officers to abide by the standards (Los Angeles Police Department, 2000: 304). Recruit officers are now required to sign for the code. All six of the existing LAPD's recruit and in-service courses (Recruit 0, Detective Supervisors, Sergeant/Civilian Supervisors, Captains, and West Point Leadership) have a section on the *Law Enforcement Code of Ethics* (Los Angeles Police Department, 2000: 306). The Board of Inquiry also recommended that every police officer receive from two to four hours of ethics and integrity every two hours.

Ethics training is important; however, there is a need to know what effect, if any, the training (ethics, academy, in-service) has on officers. Longitudinal studies are needed on the existing training programs and any created in response to scandals. Baer (1995: 8) states that it was at the New York Police Academy that "some recruits first learned about being corrupt." It was also at the academy that the recruits were introduced into the "we against them" mentality and the Blue Wall of Silence value for officers.

Finally, research is needed into the circumstances under which some officers report their fellow officers' misconduct. Researchers, myself included, have said for too long that police officers will not report fellow officers. The anecdotal evidence cited earlier seems to contradict that in some departments and for some officers. Why? If we knew the answer to that question, the police occupation would be in a better position to ensure ethical police behavior.

REFERENCES

Ahern, J. (1972). *Police in trouble: The frightening crisis in law enforcement.* New York: Hawthorne Books.

American Civil Liberties Union. (1997). *Fighting police abuse: A community action manual.* New York: American Civil Liberties Union.

Amnesty International. (1999). *United States of America: Race, rights, and police brutality.* Amnesty International-Report-AMR 51/14799. Amnesty International, New York.

Anon. (May 10, 2010). Chicago cop is accused of lying to the FBI. *Chicago Tribune.*

Anon b. (October 15, 2003). Exclusive We Content: TCLEOSE reprimand letter for Michael Meissner. *Athens Review.*

Anon c. (November 12, 2008). Two Tarpon Springs officers are under investigation. *St. Petersburg Times.*

Anon d. (May 18, 2010). Oscar Sandino, A New York City Police Department Detective was arrested on federal civil rights charges for sexual misconduct. *New York Paralegal Blog.*

Anon e. (2010). Williamston Cop forced to resign, headed for prison. News Channel 7.

Anon f. (2010). Lawtey officer accused of bribery.

Anon g. (2008). 19 cops at fault in May Day melee. The Police Policy Studies Council.

Anon h. (2006). Sex offenses most common officer misconduct. The Police Policy Studies Council.

Anon i. (2010). Tape shows tactics used to coerce false confessions. KETV 7.

Anon j. (2010). Former officer sentenced in attempted sexual assault case. KCCI.com.

Anon k. (2010). 2 city cops fired in connection with assault on paraplegic in February. Vindy.com.

Anon l. (2007). Officer used police database to blackmail victims. Mailonline.

Anon m. (2010). Male deputy awarded $35K in sexual harassment suit. ContraCosta Times.com.

Anon n. (1999). Ex-chief tells of widespread police corruption. *The New York Times.*

Anon o. (2010). Camden police corruption scandal unraveled, 185 drug cases dropped. *Times Newsline.*

Anon p. (2007). More trouble for Timoney over fee-free car deal. CBS4 News.

AP. (May 5, 2010). Ex-Customs officer imprisoned for bribery.
AP a. (May 8, 2010). Officer accused of parking in handicapped spot at Disney.
AP b. (May 3, 2010). South Carolina Sheriff Accused of Dealing Drugs From Police SUV.
AP c. (09/18/2009). Former Texas police chief arrested.
AP d. (May 13, 2010). 3 North Carolina law officers fired for off-duty trooper stop.
AP e. (5, 17, 2010). Ex-OC cop pleads guilty to sexual battery. *The Mercury News.*
AP f. (3, 23, 2009). Arizona FBI agent pleads guilty to corruption.
AP g. (2009). Former Lincoln police officer sentenced to 22 years in prison in Louisiana man's beating death.
AP h. (2010). Atlanta officer facing molestation charges. *Savannah Morning News.*
Archibold, R. C. (2009). Hired by customs. But working for Mexican Cartels. *The New York Times.*
Ascoli, D. (1979). *The Queen's peace: The origins and development of the Metropolitan Police 1829–1979.* London: Hamish Hamilton.
Atlanta Citizens Review Board. (May 13, 2010). Study and Inquiry into the Atlanta Police Department's Involvement in the Death of Ms. Kathryn Johnston.
Baer, H. (1995). Speech – The Mollen Commission and Beyond. *New York Law School Law Review 40* (1–2): 5–11.
Baker, M., & Kelley, A. (2010). Oklahoma Highway Patrol releases videos showing trooper kick women. *NewsOK.*
Banton, M. (1964). *The policeman in the community.* London: Tavistock.
Barker, J. (1999). *Danger, duty, and disillusion: The worldview of the Los Angeles police officers.* Prospect Heights, IL: Waveland Press.
Barker, T. (1977). Peer group support for police occupational deviance. *Criminology, 15* (3): 353–366.
Barker, T. (1986). White Knights, Grass Eaters, and Rogues, presented at the American Society of Criminology Annual Meeting, Atlanta, Georgia.
Barker, T. (1996). *Police ethics: Crisis in law enforcement.* Springfield, IL: Charles C Thomas.
Barker, T., Hunter, R. D., & Rush, J. P. (1994). *Police systems and practices: An introduction.* Englewood Cliffs, NJ: Prentice-Hall.
Barker, T. (2002). Ethical Police Behavior. In K. M. Lersch (Ed.), *Policing and misconduct.* Upper Saddle River, NJ: Prentice-Hall.
Barker, T., & Carter, D. L. (1994). *Police deviance* (3rd ed.). Cincinnati, OH: Anderson.
Barker, T., & Roebuck, J. (1973). *An empirical typology of police corruption: A study in organizational deviance.* Springfield, IL: Charles C Thomas.
Barrick, D. (2010). Trooper, cashier caught in ID fraud scheme. SentinelSource.com.
Bayley, D. H. (1997). The contemporary practices of policing: A comparative view. In *Civilian police and multinational peacekeeping – A workshop series: A role for democratic policing.* NIJ Research Forum, Washington, D.C., October 6, 1997, U.S. Department of Justice.
Bencks, J. (2010). Pelham trooper, 6 others charged in fraud, bribery case. *Eagle-Tribune.*

Bennetto, J. (2005). Police officers are among 22 held over quashed murder convictions. *The Independent.*

Benoit, D. (2010). Innocent man imprisoned for 19 years gets millions from city. *The Wall Street Journal.*

Biesecker, M. (2010). Trooper kills a kitty, loses his job. NorwalkReflector.com.

Blakeslee, N. (2005). *Tulia: Race, cocaine, and corruption in a small Texas town.* Public Affairs: New York.

Boyd, D. (2010). Two Fort Worth officers were drinking on duty, records show. *Star-Telegram.*

Bratton, W. J. (1995). Fighting crime as crime itself. *New York School Law Review, 40* (1–2): 35–43.

Brogden, M. (1999). Community policing as cherry pie. In R. I. Mawby (Ed.), *Policing across the world: Issues for the twenty-first century* (pp. 167–186). New York: Garland Press.

Brooks, R., & Gang, D. W. (2007). Former San Bernardino county sheriff's deputy Ivory J. Webb Jr. found not guilty of voluntary attempted manslaughter and other firearms charges. *The Press-Enterprise.*

Brown, M. K. (1981). *Working the street: Police discretion and dilemmas of reform.* New York: Russell Sage.

Carey, C. (2010). FBI agent charged with ripping off mortgage company. *The Tennessean.*

Carter, D. L. (1990). Drug related corruption of police officers: A typology. *Journal of Criminal Justice, 18* (2): 85–89.

Carter, D. L., & Stephens, D. W. (1991). An overview of issues concerning police officer drug use. In T. Barker & D. L. Carter (Eds.), *Police deviance* (2nd ed.). Cincinnati, OH: Anderson.

Carver, L. G. (May 5, 2010). Ex-Slaton officer found guilty. *Avelanche-Journal.*

CBSNEWS. (July 4, 2004). Targeted in Tulia, Texas?: Former undercover drug agent tells his story to 60 Minutes.

Chevigny, P. (1969). *Police power: Police abuses in New York City.* New York: Panthenon Books.

Christopher, W. (1991). The Independent Commission on the Los Angeles Police Department. *Report of the Independent Commission on the Los Angeles Police Department.* Los Angeles: City of Los Angeles.

Collom, L. (2010). Former Mesa cop convicted of child molestation. *The Arizona Republic.*

Commission on Police Integrity. (1997). *Report of the Commission on Police Integrity.* Presented to the City of Chicago, Richard M. Daley Mayor. Chicago: City of Chicago.

Conte, M. (May 1, 2010). Jersey City cop sentenced to prison for assault on girlfriend, endangering child. *The Jersey Journal.*

Conte, M. (2010). Jury awards $760,000 to Old Bridge woman who accused 2 NJ Transit cops of rape in Liberty State Park. NJ.com.

Cote, J. G. (2010). Two in court in alleged sticker scam. Nashuatelegraph.com.

Coulson, R. (1993). *Police under pressure: Resolving disputes.* Westport, CT: Greenwood Press.

Crank, J. P. (1998). *Understanding police culture.* Cincinnati, OH: Anderson Press.
Crockett, P. (2010). Former ATF agent pleads guilty in Tulsa federal court. KRMG Local News.
Curran, K. (2010). I-Team: Trooper caught parking in handicapped spot. CBS Broadcasting.
Dale, M. (2010). DA: Pa. Officer raped, assaulted girls in his care. AP.
Davis, M. (1997). Teaching police ethics: What to aim at. In J. Kleing & M. L. Smith (Eds.), *Teaching criminal justice ethics: Strategic issues* (pp. 35–85). Cincinnati, OH: Anderson.
Delattre, E. (1989). *Character and cops: Ethics in policing.* Washington, DC: Anderson.
Department of Justice. (06/08/09). DOJ Headline Archives Abuse of Trust: The Case of the Crooked Border Official.
Dienst, J. (2009). NYPD officer accused of helping drug gang. www.nbcnewyork.com.
Dobyns, J., & Johnson-Shelton, N. (2009). *No angel: My harrowing undercover journey to the inner circle of the Hells Angels.* New York: Crown.
Dolnick, S. (2009). Kerik confesses to cheating I.R.S. and telling lies. *The New York Times.*
Donnelly, F. (2010). 8 years in prison for Arden Heights sea cadets instructor accused of molesting teens. Silive.com.
DOJ Office of Public Affairs. (December 15, 2009). Two Shenandoah Men and Four Police Officers Indicted for Hate Crime and Related Corruption.
DOJ Press Release. (March 12, 2008). Former Pennsylvania State Trooper Federally Charged.
DOJ Press Release. (March 06, 2009). Two Former NYPD Detectives Who Secretly Worked as Mafia Associates Sentenced to Life Imprisonment for Racketeering and Murder.
DOJ Press Release. (March 18, 2009). Federal Jury Convicts Ex-FBI Agent and Accomplice in Scheme to Commit Violent Home-Invasion Robbery.
DOJ Press Release. (April 28, 2009). San Diego Police Officer Pleads Guilty to Misusing Position to Help Drug Traffickers.
DOJ Press Release. (June 5, 2009). Airport Police Officer Convicted of Selling Cocaine Sentenced to Prison.
DOJ Press Release. (July 1, 2009). Former Memphis Police Officer Sentenced to Prison Term of Life Plus 255 Years for Civil Rights, Narcotics, Robbery, and Firearms Charges.
DOJ Press Release. (July 30, 2009). Former Massachusetts State Trooper Sentenced on Conspiracy and Cocaine Distribution Charges.
DOJ Press Release. (November, 2009). Former Memphis, Tennessee Police Officer Sentenced to 27 Months in Prison for Civil Rights Violations.
DOJ Press Release. (November 23, 2009). Former U.S. Immigration Officer Pleads Guilty to Destroying Government Files and Producing a False Immigration Document.
DOJ Press Release. (June 10, 2009). Former Benton Harbor Police Officer Sentenced after Pleading Guilty to Felony Drug Offense.

DOJ Press Release. (January 22, 2010). Former Customs and Border Protection Officer Sentenced to Federal Prison.

DOJ Press Release. (February 24, 2010). Harris County Deputy Sheriff indicted for Disclosing Confidential Information for Cash.

DOJ Press Release. (February 24, 2010). Former New Orleans Police Officer Pleads Guilty to Conspiring to Cover Up the Danziger Bridge Shootings.

DOJ Press Release. (March 11, 2010). Houston Jury Convicts Former Conroe Police Officer of Bank Robbery.

DOJ Press Release. (March 30, 2010). New Orleans Officer Charged in Danziger Bridge Case.

DOJ Press Release. (April 16, 2010). Fourth New Orleans Police Officer Charged in Danziger Bridge Case.

DOJ Press Release. (April 20, 2010). Second NYPD Officer Pleads Guilty in Perfume Warehouse Armed Robber Scheme.

DOJ Press Release. (May 18, 2010). Ex-Passaic County Sheriff's Department Detective-Sergeant Gets 85 Months for Conspiring to Steal Cocaine from Evidence Vault. USDA's Office District of New Jersey.

DOJ Press Release. (May 5, 2010). Santa Cruz County Deputy Arrested for Drug Smuggling. USDA's Office District of Arizona.

DOJ Press Release. (June 3, 2010). Former Liquor Enforcement Officer changes Pleas Mid-Trial. USDA's Office Eastern District of Pennsylvania.

DOJ Press Release. (June 3, 2010). Former Police Officer Charged with $889,000 Ponzi Scheme. USDA's Office Northern District of Ohio.

DOJ Press Release. (June 3, 2010). IRS Agent Charged with Accepting a Bribe. USDA's Office District of Minnesota.

DOJ Press Release. (June 3, 2010). Border Patrol Agent Pleads Guilt to Civil Rights Violations. Office of Public Affairs.

DOJ Press Release. (June 4, 2010). Fifth New Orleans Police Officer Pleads Guilty in Danziger Bridge Case. USDA's Eastern District of Louisiana.

DOJ Press Release. (June 4, 2010). Former Florence County Deputy Sentenced to 400 Years' Imprisonment. USDA's District of South Carolina.

DOJ Press Release. (June 9, 2010). Fort Lauderdale Attorney Sentenced to 50 Years in Billion-Dollar Ponzi Scheme.

DOJ Press Release. (June 10, 2010). USDA's Eastern District of New York.

DOJ Press Release. (June 11, 2010). Five Current and Former New Orleans Police Officers Charged in the Shooting and Burning of a New Orleans Man in the Days After Hurricane Katrina. U.S Department of Justice Office of Public Affairs.

Dulai, S. (2010). On-duty HPD officer accused of sex assaults. *Houston Chronicle.*

Eldeib, D. (2010). Man wins $1.3M in malicious prosecution case. Chicagotribune.com.

Eligon, J, (2010). Ex-officer is convicted on charges of sex abuse. *The New York Times.*

Estep, T. (2010). Former officer indicted in Taser incident. Gwinnettdailypost.com.

Faulk, K. (June 13, 2010). Alabama troopers at Birmingham post instructed to cite more for DUI. Al.com.

FBI. (2010). Headline Archives. Combating Border Corruption: Locally and nationally.
Ferraresi, M. (2010). Phoenix police accuse officer of stealing from drug dealers. *The Arizona Republic.*
Finney, D. (2010). Former Des Moines officer will appeal firing, attorney says. *Des Moines Register.*
Fisher, J., & Weiss, M. (May 6, 2010). NYPD cop charged for role in trafficking ring. *New York Post.*
Fogelson, R. M. (1977). *Big city police.* Cambridge, MA: Harvard University Press.
Frownfelder, D. (2010). Deputy's ride home leads to discipline. *Daily Telegram.*
Fullbright, L. (2010). Tulsa police investigation prompts lawsuit. NewOn6.com.
Funk, J. (2010). Ex-CSI chief gets prison for evidence tampering. WKRN.com.
Gaines, L. K., & Kappeler, V. E. (1992). The police selection process: What works? In G. Cordner & D. Hale (Eds.), *What works in policing? Operations and administration examined* (pp. 107–124). Cincinnati, OH: Anderson.
Gillham, O. (2010). Drug bust fraud alleged. *Tulsa World.*
Gillham, O., & Harper, D. (2010). Ex-ATF agent charged in indictment. *Tulsa World.*
Gladden, M. (2010). Neptune OKs $65G settlement with Brick man. APP.com.
Greenfield, L. A., Lanagen, P. A., & Smith, S. K. (1997). *Police use of force: Collection of national data.* Washington, DC: U.S. Department of Justice: GPO.
Haas, E. (2006). Police misconduct: A preponderance of perjury. *The Muckraker Report.*
Haggard, P. (1994). *Police ethics.* Lewiston, NY: Edwin Mellen Press.
Hall, R. (2010). Former Paw Paw police officer, gym owner arraigned on drug charges related to steroids. *Kalamazoo News.*
Hatzipanagos, R. (2010). Monroe county sheriff's deputy charged with fondling boy, 15. OrlandoSentinel.com.
Hays, T. (2010). NY to pay "Mafia cop" victim record $9.9 million. *U.S. News.*
Heffernan, S. (2009). Spring Lake residents look for answers amid police probe. WRAL.com.
Heffernan, W. C. (1985). The police and their rules of office: An ethical analysis. In W. C. Heffernan & T. Stroup (Eds.), *Police ethics: Hard choices in law enforcement* (pp. 3–24). New York: John Jay Press.
Heffernan, W. C. (1996). Rejoinders: William C. Heffernan and John Kleing. In J. Kleing & M. L. Smith (Eds.), *Teaching criminal justice: Strategic issues* (pp. 25–34). Cincinnati, OH: Anderson.
Hendon, J. (2010). State appellate court rejects former Lincoln officer appeal. *Birmingham Crime Examiner.*
Herbert, S. (1997). *Policing space: Territoriality and the Los Angeles Police Department.* Minneapolis, MN: University of Minnesota Press.
Hetherman, B. (2010). *City News Service.*
Hoffman, P. (1993). The feds, lies and videotape: The need for an effective federal role in controlling police abuse in urban America. *Southern California Law Review, 66* (4); 1455–1531.
Holdaway, S. (1984). *Inside the British Police: A force at work.* New York: Basil Blackwell.

Hopkins, E. J. (1972). *Our lawless police: A study in the unlawful enforcement of the laws.* New York: DeCapo Press. (First published in 1931).

Hoy, V. L. (1982). Research and Planning. In Garmire (Ed.), *Local government public management* (2nd ed.). Washington, DC: International City Management Association.

Hughes, M. (2009). Police officers charges over "Cardiff Three" miscarriage of justice. *The Independent.*

Human Rights Watch. (1998). *Shielded from justice.* New York: Human Rights Watch.

International Association of Chiefs of Police. (1981). *Police ethics.* Training Key 295. Gaithersburg, MD: IACP.

International Association of Chiefs of Police. (1997). *Model policy: Standards of conduct.* Alexandria, VA: IACP National Law Enforcement Policy Center.

James, R. (2009). Bernard Kerik. *Time.*

Kalinowski, B. (2009). Shenandoah police chief accused of cover-up ordered held. *Republican Herald.*

Kamm, F. M. (1997). Response to Callahan and Whitbeck: Practical ethics, moral theories, and deliberation. In J. Kleing & M. L. Smith (Eds.), *Teaching criminal justice ethics: Strategic issues* (pp. 123–130). Cincinnati, OH: Anderson.

Kania, R. E. (1988). Should we tell police to say "Yes" to Gratuities? *Criminal Justice Ethics 7*(2): 37–49.

Kappeler, V. E., Sluder, R. D., & Alpert, G. P. (1994). *Forces of deviance: The dark side of policing.* Prospect Heights, IL: Waveland Press.

Kapitan, C. (2010). Ex-police officer handed probation. *Express-News.*

Katz, M. (2010). Camden police scandal has widespread consequences. Philly.com.

Kleing, J. (1996). *The ethics of policing.* Cambridge, MA: Cambridge University Press.

Klockers, C. B. (1980). The Dirty Harry problem. *The Annals. 452* (November): 34–47.

Knapp Commission. (1973). *The Knapp Commission Report on Police Corruption.* New York: George Braziller.

Kraska, P. B. (1996). Enjoying militarism: Political/personal dilemmas in studying U.S. Police paramilitary units. *Justice Quarterly, 12* (1): 85–111.

Kramer, J. (2010). Mobile County sheriff's deputy fired after allegedly extorting money from illegal immigrants. *Press Register.*

Lane, R. (1971). *Policing the city: Boston 1822–1885.* New York: Antheneum.

Lee, M. W. L. (1971). *A history of police in England.* Montclair, NJ: Patterson Smith Reprint. (First published in 1901).

Lehr, D. (2009). *The fence: A police cover-up along Boston's racial divide.* New York: HarperCollins.

Leuci, R. (2004). *All the centurions.* New York: William Morrow.

Livingstone, D. (1977). Police discretion and the quality of life in public places: Courts, Communities, and the new policing. *Columbia Law Review, 97*(3): 551–672.

Lord, R. (May 5, 2010). Ravenstahl to public safety workers: Clean up your act. *Pittsburg Post Gazette.*

Los Angeles Police Department. (2000). *Board of Inquiry into the Rampart area corruption incident: Public report.* Los Angeles: LAPD.

Macdonald, C., & Wilkinson, M. (2010), Detroit police misdeeds to big payouts. Chicagotribune.com.
Martinez, M. (2009). Lawsuits vs. cops costing $30 M to settle. CBS.
Marx, G. T. (1985). Police undercover work: Ethical deception or deceptive ethics. In W. C. Heffernan & T. Stroup (Eds.), *Police ethics: Hard choices in law enforcement* (pp. 83–115). New York: John Jay Press.
Massini, H. J. (1985). Preface. In W. C. Heffernan & T. Stroup (Eds.), *Police ethics: Hard choices in law enforcement* (pp. i–ix). New York: John Jay Press.
Masterson, T. (2010). FOP throws party for reinstated cops in beating case. Philadelphia.
McAlary, M. (1994). *Good cop, bad cop.* New York: Pocket Books.
McCullagh, D. (2008). *Customs agent took bribes to access Fed police database.* CNET.
McDonald, J. (May 12, 2010). Ex-Scranton police officer in trouble again. Thetimestribune.com.
McDonald, P. P., Gaffigan, S. J., & Greenberg, S. J. (1997). Police Integrity: Definition and historical significance. In S. J. Gaffigan & P. P. McDonald (project managers). *Police integrity: Public service with honor* (pp. 81–91). Washington, DC: GPO.
McKinney, M. (2010). Minneapolis settles suit with man who alleged police beating. StarTribune.com.
Melzer, E. J. a. (2009). Benton Harbor narcotics chief pleads guilty to conspiracy. *The Michigan Messenger.*
Melzer, E. J. b. (2009). Drug cases dismissed following pleas by corrupt. . . *The Michigan Messenger.*
Miller, W. R. (1997). *Cops and Bobbies: Police authority in New York and London, 1830–1870* (2nd ed.). Columbus, OH: Ohio State University Press.
Mims, B. (2009). Spring Lake officials back probe of department. Capitol Broadcasting Company.
Mollen Commission. (1994). *The City of New York Commission to Investigate Allegations of Police Corruption and the Anti-Corruption Procedures of the Police Department: Commission Report.* New York: City of New York.
Moore, M. (1997). Epilogue. In S. J. Gaffigan & P. P. McDonald (project managers). *Police integrity: Public service with honor* (pp. 59–70). Washington, DC: GPO.
Moore, M. (May 1, 2010). Deputy ousted in porn scandal. *The Daily Item.*
Moritz, O. (2010). Disgraced ex-top cop Bernard Kerik becomes inmate number 84888-054 in Maryland federal prison. *New York Daily News.*
Mulick, S. (2010). Tacoma police officer charged with child molestation. *The News Tribune.*
Mulvihill, G. (2010). Residents of New Jersey city say cops worse than criminals. *Deseret News.*
National Advisory Commission on Criminal Justice Standards and Goals. (1973). *The police.* Washington, DC: GPO.
Nelson, D. (1995). Cops' free rein costs city millions. *Chicago Tribune,* January 10.
Nelson, P. (2010). Cop found guilty of drug charges. www.timesunion.com.
News4jax.com. (2010). 2 Fla cops arrested for alleged false incident reports.

Nielson, G. (2007). Probable cause found in Timoney fee free car deal. CBS4 News.
Nielson, J. (January 2, 2010). Accusations fly in feud involving Texas lawmen, porn charges. *The Dallas Morning Star*.
Ostrom, E., Parks, R., & Whitaker, G. (1978). *Patterns of metropolitan policing*. Cambridge, MA: Ballinger.
Ovalle, D. (2009). Timoney loses free SUV-probe appeal. *Miami Herald*.
Perez, E. S. (2010). Texas police chief near border faces drug charges. AP.
Pistone, J. D. (1987). *Donnie Brasco: My undercover life in the Mafia*. New York: Nail Books.
Queen, W. (2005). *Under and alone*. New York: Random House.
Reith, C. (1952). *The blind eye of history: A study of the origins of the present police era*. Montclair, NJ: Patterson Smith.
Reynolds, E. A. (1998). *Before the Bobbies: The night watch and police reform in Metropolitan London, 1720–1830*. Stanford, CA: Stanford University Press.
Richardson, J. F. (1974). *Urban police in the United States*. Port Washington, NY: Kennikat Press.
Robilliard, St., J., & McEwan, J. (1986). *Police powers and the individual*. New York: Basil Blackwell.
Roebuck, J. Arrests part of nationwide drug sting. *The Monitor*.
Rogers, J. (2009). Former Lake City police officer to appeal 20-year federal sentence. SCNow.com.
Rubinstein, J. (1973). *City police*. New York: Strauss & Giroux.
Sapp, A. (1994). Sexual misconduct by police officers. In T. Barker & D. L. Carter (Eds.), *Police deviance* (3rd ed.) (pp. 187–200). Cincinnati, OH: Anderson.
Schecter, L., & Phillips, W. (1973). *On the pad*. New York: Putnam.
Schoettler, J. (2010). Jacksonville police sergeant charged after suspect's beating. Jacksonville.com.
Schoichet, C. E. (2010). New Orleans mayor asks feds to review city police force. Cnn.com.
Scolforo, M. (2008). Feds Charge Ex-Pa. Trooper in Pimp Case. AP Online.
Sherman, A., Weaver, J., & Lebovich, J. (2009). Fed: Rothstein showered high-ranking officers with 'gratuities.' *The Miami Herald*.
Sherman, L. (1978). *Scandal and reform: Controlling police corruption*. Berkeley, CA: University of California Press.
Simmons, A. (2009). Waffle House waiter sues over Taser incident. *Atlanta Journal Constitution*.
Skolnick, J. (1966). *Justice without trial*. New York: John Wiley.
Skolnick, J. (1982). Deception by Police. *Criminal Justice Ethics, 1*(2): 40–50.
Smith, L. (2010). Charges dropped in lawyer's Five Points arrest, officers refuse to testify. www.wistv.com.
SPD Citizens Review Panel. (1999). *Seattle Police Department: Citizens Review Panel Final Report*. Seattle, WA: City of Seattle.
Staff. (2010). Sheriff's deputy fired following alleged assault in Montgomery County. Tennessean.com.
Stanforth, L. (2010). Ex-Schenectady cop sentenced for incident that cost his job. *Times Union*.

Stitt, B. G., & James, G. G. (1985). Entrapment an ethical analysis. In F. A. Elliston & Feldberg (Eds.), *Moral issues in police work*. Totowa, NJ: Rowan and Allanhand.

Sugimotot, M. (2010). Deputy sheriff pleads guilty to assaulting child. *Hawaii News Now*.

Sulzberger, A. G. (May 13, 2010). One officer seeks bail as ex-officer pleads guilty. *Times-Picayune*.

(May 7, 2010). New Orleans' new police chief, Ronal Serpas: An editorial.

Swickard, J. (2010). Cop gets probation for misconduct. *Free Press*.

Terribone, A. (2010). Brandon Jay McFadden pleads guilty to drug conspiracy.

Trexler, P. (2010). Steroid probe targets two more Akron officers. *Beacon Journal*.

Travis, J. (1998). *Plenary Address at the Fourth Biennial Conference: International Perspectives on Crime, Justice, and Public Order*. Budapest, Hungary.

U.S. Department of Justice. (1978). *Prevention, Detection, and Correction of Corruption In Local Government*. Washington, DC: Department of Justice.

U.S. Department of Justice. (2010). Three Baltimore City Police Department Officers convicted in civil rights case. PR Newswire.

U.S. Government Accounting Office. (1998). *Law Enforcement: Information on Drug-Related Police Corruption*. Report to the Honorable Charles B. Rangel, House of Representatives. Washington, DC: GPO.

Vera, (1998). *Prosecuting police misconduct: Reflections on the role of the U.S. Civil Rights Division*. New York: Vera Institute of Justice.

Vicchio, S. J. (1997). *Ethics and Police Integrity: Some Definitions and Questions for Study*. Key Note Address, Police Integrity: Police Service with Honor, January, 1997, National Institute of Justice and the Office of Community Oriented Police Service.

Vielmetti, B. (March 26, 2010). State drug agent arrested in sting. *Milwaukee Journal Sentinel*.

Vollmer, A. (1971). *The police and modern society*. Montclair, NJ: Patterson Smith. (First published in 1936).

Walker, S. (1977). *A critical history of policing: The emergence of professionalism*. Lexington, MA: Lexington Books.

Walker, S. (1983). *The police in America*. New York: McGraw-Hill.

Wallman, B. (2010). City suspends Fort Lauderdale police officers who ran Rothstein detail. *The Sun Sentinel*.

Wellborn, L. (2009). Former CHP officer guilty of attempted lewd conduct. *The Orange County Register*.

Welfel, E. J. (1997). Psychology's contribution to effective models of ethics education in criminal justice. In J. Kleing & M. L. Smith (Eds.), *Teaching criminal justice ethics: Strategic issues* (pp. 131–152). Cincinnati, OH: Anderson.

Witham, D. C. (1985). *The American law enforcement chief executive: A management profile*. Washington, DC: Police Executive Research Forum.

WLEX-18. (2009). Deputy pleads guilty to murder facilitation.

Wren, T. E. (1985). Whistle-blowing and loyalty to one's friends. In W. C. Heffernan & T. Stroup (Eds.), *Police ethics: Hard choices in law enforcement* (pp. 25–43). New York: John Jay Press.

INDEX

A

abuse of authority. *See also* police brutality
   conviction of the innocent, 120–125
   definition, 9, 107
   forms of, 107
   lies for perceived legitimate goals, 118–120
   noble cause injustice, 113–118
   punishment for, 37–38
   supervisors' role, 130
   use of force, 108–113
acceptance of gratuities, 33–34
accepted lying, 40–43
accountability, 141–142
active cooperation, 74
Adderley, Frank, 51
administrative reaction, 133–134
administrative weapon, 133–134
admission standards, 12
aggressive police tactics, 108–113
Alabama's Ethics Commission, 47–48, 49
alcoholism, 140
Alford, LaRue, 83, 84
All the Centurions, 62
American Civil Liberties Union (ACLU), 112, 142
American Criminal Justice System, 113–114
Americans with Disabilities Act, 140
Amnesty International, 112, 132, 142
anonymous complaints, 104–105
Anti-Corruption Manual for Administrators in Law Enforcement, 91
anticorruption policy, 87
anti-prostitution patrol, 6
arbitration, 47, 80
arrest powers, 20–21

assault. *See* police brutality
assaulting arrests. *See* police brutality
Atlanta, Georgia, 7–8
Atlanta Citizen Review Board (ACRB), 123–124, 125
Atlanta Police Department, 123–124, 125
auditing behavior, 131
audits, 142
authority abuse. *See* abuse of authority

B

background checks, 78, 138, 140, 558
"bad apple" defense, 125
Baer, H., 146
bank fraud, 29
Barker, Joan, 128
Barker, T., 60
Barker's typology of police corruption. *See* patterns of police corruption
bars, 91–93
behavior, deviant, 35–36
behavior audit, 131
behavior of police officers, 26–27
Benjamin, David, 51
Benton Harbor, Michigan Police Department, 84
Birmingham News, 124
Birmingham Six, 120
Black's Law Dictionary, 41
Blue Rats, 128
Blue Wall of Silence. *See* code of silence
Board of Inquiry, 145–146
border agents, 6
border control inspectors, 6
Border Corruption Task Forces, 72
Boston Police Department, 69

bottle clubs, 91–93
Bradley-Wragg, Juanita Cunningham, 83
Bratton, William, 69, 110
bribery, 63–65, 66–67
British police officers, 112–113, 115–116, 127
Brown, M. K., 114
brutality. *See* police brutality
"Buddy Boys" scandal, 63
Building Integrity and Reducing Drug Corruption in Police Departments, 103–104

C

cabarets, 91–93
cabs, 96–97
Camden, 81–82
Camden cops, 122
Canons of Police Ethics, 46–47
Caracappa, Steven, 121
Cardiff Three, 121
Carlson, Dan, 15
Carter, D. L., 38, 69, 80, 117
certification, 135–136
Chicago Commission on Police Integrity, 131
Chicago corruption scandal, 77
child molestation, 28
Christopher Commission, 132
citizen arrest powers, 21
citizen complaints, 133–134
citizen-initiated sexual contacts, 57
citizen-police cooperation, 74
citizen-police encounters, 107–108, 111
city regulation violations, 66
civilian review boards, 142
civil liberties, 23, 117
Civil Rights Division, 4, 113, 141
civil rights violations, 141
civil suit, 130, 137
clubs, 91–93
Code of Ethics. *See* Law Enforcement Code of Ethics
code of silence, 105, 127–128, 140, 146
coercive interference, 10–11
Coleman, Tom, 136–137
command review, 132
complaints, 104–105, 133–134
Compstats, 133–134

conduct, 28, 89
confidentiality, 30
consent decree, 141
constables' working rules, 113
constitutional restraints, 10
constitutional rights, 2, 24
constitutional violations, 117
Constitution and Bill of Rights, 23–24, 141
construction sites, 93–94
contacts, 53–56
"contempt of cop," 31
continuum of officers in corrupt departments, 85
control systems
    administrative reaction, 133–134
    departmental, 76
    early warning audit systems, 131–133
    external accountability, 141–142
    external review boards, 142
    internal discipline, 80
    internal v. external, 126
    peer group control, 127–130
    self-control, 126–127
    supervisory control, 130
    technical assists, 132–133
conviction of the innocent, 120–125
core values, 127
corruption, 37–38, 62–63. *See also* patterns of police corruption
    definition and elements, 60
corruption control. *See also* corruption prevention
    approaches to, 144
    decreasing the opportunity, 87–88
    external review boards, 142
    increased supervision, 91
    policy, 88
    public education, 90
    sustained action, 9
    use of peer group, 102–106
corruption locations, 105
corruption patrols, 105
corruption prevention, 88–89. *See also* corruption control
corrupt officers, 74–78
corrupt police departments
    continuum of officers in, 85
    examples of, 81–85
    types of officers, 85–87

Coulson, R., 128
cover-up misconduct, 141
cover-ups, 6–7, 7–8, 44–45
crime-fighter model, 112
crimes, 6, 62, 65, 69–70
criminal activities, 67–72, 75
criminal case fixes, 66–67
criminal enterprises, 50–51
criminal investigation, 21
Criminal Justice System, 22, 36
criminal law enforcement officers, 6. *See also* police misconduct
crisis, ethical. *See* ethical crisis
Crispin, Margarita, 6
Crispin Case, 6
culture of retaliation, 129
Customs and Border Enforcement, 80

D

Danza, Tony, 26
Danziger Bridge, 44–45
Danziger shootings, 7
dash cams, 133
Davis, Len, 86, 106
Daytona, Florida, 47
deadly force, 108, 112
deceptive practices, 40–42
decertification, 115, 135–136. *See also* loss of certification
Decision-making processes, 27
defense of entrapment, 41–42
Delattre, E., 51, 76, 79
demonstrators, 110
departmental control systems, 76
Department of Homeland Security, 80
Department of Justice, 26, 113, 141
deviant behavior, 35–36
deviant lying, 43–45
direct criminal activities, 67–72, 75
direct police services, 20, 21
disabilities, 140
discipline, 133
discretion, 31–32
discretionary decision-making, 85
discriminatory treatment, 142
dishonorably discharges, 138
disinformation, 42–43
Dobyns, Jay, 40

domestic violence convictions, 27
Dowd, Michael, 46
Dowd Test, 46
drinking on duty, 38
drug addiction, 116
drug cartels, 81
drug dealers, 65
drug enforcement, 89–90, 119–120
drug-related corruption, 68–70, 72
drug-related crimes, 6, 7, 116–118
drug trafficking, 6
drug use, 38–39, 99–101, 116–118
drunk driving arrests, 27
DUI shakedown (costs of), 64–65

E

early warning system, 103–104, 131–133, 142
education of the public, 90
employment records, 139–140
entrapment, 41–42
Eppolito, Louis, 121
erroneous information, 42–43
ethical behavior, 11–12
ethical crisis, 8
ethical principles, 15, 17–18
ethical violations, 143–144
ethics definition, 15, 19
ethics training, 145–146
ethnographic study, 129
evidence, 133
excessive force, 3. *See also* use of force
external accountability, 141–142
external control, 126, 130–131
external reaction, 37
extortion, 63–65, 69–70, 72–73, 81
extreme positions, 85

F

falsely arrested, 4
favors. *See* gratuities
Federal Bureau of Investigations, 72
felony fixes, 66–67
field supervision, 131
fixes, 66–67, 75
flaunting one's position, 29–30
Florida Civil Rights Act, 140

force (use of). *See* use of force
Fort Lauderdale, Florida, 50–51
fragmented law enforcement, 22
framing innocent people, 120–125
Frank, Antoinette, 79–80
fraud, 29
Freeh, Louis, 87

G

gambling, 99
garages, 95–96
general discharge, 137
Georgia, Atlanta, 7–8
Gibbs, Barry, 121
gifts. *See* gratuities
grass eaters, 75, 86
gratuities
    and Alabama Ethics Commission, 49
    and Canons of Police Ethics, 46–47
    and corruption, 45–46
    and the Law Enforcement Code of Ethics, 33–34, 48
    mandatory reporting practices, 51–52
    and organized crime groups, 50–51
    police officers demanding, 47
    public education, 90
    value/nature of gifts, 47–48, 49–50
Great Britain police. *See* British police officers
grills, 91–93
group solidarity, 101
group support (undermining), 101–102
guiding principles, 88
Guildford Four, 120
gypsy cabs, 96–97
gypsy cops
    decertification, 134–136
    definition, 56, 134
    examples, 134, 136–137
    explanation for, 140
    separation of licensee, 137–138
    terminations/resignations, 135–136
    in Tulia, Texas, 121–122

H

"hand offs," 124
harassment, 52–53, 58
hazards
    bars, grills, cabarets and bottle clubs, 91
    construction sites, 93
    gambling, 99
    gypsy or unlicensed cabs, 96
    hotels and restaurants, 94
    narcotics, 99–100
    parking lots, 95
    prostitution, 98
    repair shops, garages, trucking companies, 95
    tow trucks, 97
    traffic violations, 97
head-mounted cameras, 133
Heffernan, W. C., 114
Herbert, S., 114
Hobbs Act extortion, 65
Hoffman, P., 112
Holdaway, S., 115, 127
home invasions, 69
homeland security, 71–72, 80
honorably discharged, 137
Hopkins, Ernest Jerome, 113–114
Hoskins, John, 138, 139–140
hotels, 94–95
human growth hormones, 39
Hurricane Katrina, 44–45

I

ideal police force, 10
illegal activities, protection of, 65–67
illegal immigrants, 6, 64, 71–72, 81
illegitimate goals, 43–45
Immigrants Rights May Day, 110
immigration documents, 71–72
immoral acts, 45
improper sexual contact. *See* sexual misconduct
increased supervision, 91
indecent exposure, 53
indicators of problem
    construction sites, 93
    hotels and restaurants, 94
    narcotics, 100
    parking lots, 95
    prostitution, 98
    repair shops, garages, trucking companies, 95–96

tow trucks, 97–98
traffic violations, 97
individual rights, 23
informants, 128–129
informer, 128
integrity, 29
integrity tests, 105–106
internal affairs investigation, 113
internal affairs unit, 102, 103–105, 105–106
internal control, 126–127
internal discipline system, 80
Internal payoffs, 72–73, 75
internal policing, 102–105
internal reaction, 38, 39
International Association of Chiefs of Police (IACP), 12, 17, 51, 103–104
Internet sexual predators, 28–29
interviews, 105–106
intoxicated police officers, 38
invalid traffic stop, 53
investigations, 133

J

Johnston, Kathryn, 123–124, 125, 128
Josephenson, Michael, 47
Josephenson Institute for Ethics, 47
Justice Department. *See* U.S. Department of Justice
justification. *See* rationalization

K

Kania, R. E., 45, 46
Kerik, Bernard, 49–50
kickbacks, 61, 75
King, Rodney, 8, 112, 132, 141
Knapp Commission, 75–76
"knock and talk" techniques, 117

L

Lake City, South Carolina Corruption, 82–84
law enforcement, 9, 10, 12, 23
Law Enforcement Code of Ethics
    acceptance of gratuities, 33–34
    and constitutional rights, 23–24
    and corruption control, 89
    current version, 16–17
    definition, 20
    ethical training, 145
    exposing corrupt cops, 129
    and gratuities, 48
    honest in thought and deed, 29
    and master status, 25–26
    personal commitment and responsibility, 36
    and police lying, 39–40
    purpose, 15
    serve, protect, and respect, 21
Law Enforcement Ethics Center of the Southwestern Law Enforcement Institute, 145
Law Enforcement Oath of Honor, 17
law enforcement officers
    abuse of powers or position, 29–30, 51–52
    and the Criminal Justice System, 22
    definition, 20–21
    in Great Britain, 112–113, 115–116
    gypsy cops (*see* gypsy cops)
    peer pressure, 101
    and personal feelings, 31
    quotas, 124–125, 130
    screening process, 126–127
    stress, 103
    testimony, 119
    and their personal lives, 26–27
    types of, 85–87
lawsuits
    civil, 130, 137
    pattern-or-practice concept, 141–142
    against police, 143–144
    Tennessee v. Garner, 112
    USA v Scott Rothstein, 50–51
Lee, M. W. L., 10
legal abuse, 107
legal guilt, 118
legal restraints, 10
legal restrictions, 6
Leuci, Robert, 62
license restrictions, 66
limited authority, 22
local control, 22
London Metropolitan Police, 9, 49
Los Angeles, California, 8
Los Angeles Police Department (LAPD), 8, 77–79, 110, 128, 145
Los Angeles Rampart Area, 76

loss of certification, 52. *See also* decertification
loyalty, 127–128, 130
Luchese crime family, 69, 121
lying. *See* police lying

M

Mafia, 50–51
Mafia cops, 69, 121
management oversight, 130–131
management tool, 133–134
Marx, G. T., 40–41
Masini, Hugo, 76
master status, 25–26
McCaster, Kenneth, 82–83
McCormack, Robert, 91
McKnight, Shanita, 70, 82, 84
meat eaters, 75–76, 86
media and police lying, 42
Meissner, Michael, 138, 139
Metropolitan Police Act, 9
Metropolitan Police Department, 79, 129
Mexican drug cartels, 81
Miami, Florida, 79
Miami Civilian Investigative Panel, 50
Miami-Dade Ethics Commission, 50
Miami Police Department, 50
minorities dealings, 9, 111–112
misdemeanor fixes, 66–67
misuse of computers, 58–59
molestation, 28
Mollen, Milton, 134
Mollen Commission, 69, 76–77, 119–120, 131, 134
monitoring, 141
moral decision-making, 130
morality v. ethics, 15, 19
motorcycle gangs/clubs, 40
Murphy, Patrick, 76

N

narcotics, 99–101
narcotics and/or drug enforcement, 89–90
National Advisory Commission on Criminal Justice Standards and Goals, 23
National Association for the Advancement of Colored People, 112
New Jersey, 81–82

New Jersey's Attorney General Office, 141–142
New Orleans, Louisiana, 6–7
New Orleans Police Department (NOPD), 6–7, 44–45, 79–80, 81
New York City corruption scandal, 75–76
New York Police Department, 46, 63, 69, 76–77, 86
New York Times, 80
Noble Cause Injustice
   convicting the innocent, 120–125
   explanation, 113–116
   lies for perceived legitimate goals, 118–120
   need for elimination, 144
   in the war on drugs, 7, 84, 116–118
nomadic cops. *See* gypsy cops
nonlethal weapons, 4–5
nonsexual contact, 52–53

O

Oath of Honor, 17
objective test, 41
occupational culture, 127, 143
occupational subculture, 128
off-duty behavior, 26–27, 60
officers' conduct. *See* police conduct
official reports, 120
O. J. Simpson trial, 118–119
Operation Deliverance, 81
Operation Shattered Shield, 6
opportunistic crimes, 74
opportunistic thefts, 61–63, 75
organizational/rule violations
   accepting gratuities (*see* gratuities)
   drinking on duty, 38
   external/internal reactions, 37–38
   and police lying (*see* police lying)
   use of drugs, 38–39
organized crime groups, 50–51
Oswald, Lee Harvey, 26

P

paranoia, 103, 104
parking lots, 95
passive cooperation, 74
patrol, 21
pattern-or-practice civil suits, 141–142

patterns of police corruption. *See also* corruption
   acts and organizations, 75t
   direct criminal activities, 67–72, 75
   fixes, 66–67, 75
   internal payoffs, 72–73, 75
   kickbacks, 61, 75
   opportunistic thefts, 61–63, 75
   protection of illegal activities, 65–67, 75
   shakedowns, 63–65, 75
patterns of social interaction, 127
payoffs, 72–73, 75
peace officers, 135
Peace Officers Standard and Training Council (POST), 52
pedophiles, 28–29
peer group pressure, 101
perceived legitimate goals, 43, 118–120
Perez, Rafael, 77, 86
performance standards, 13
perjury, 43–44, 113–115, 119–120
Perry, Rick, 137
personal commitment, 36
personal feelings of officers, 31
personal information, 139–140
personal lives of officers, 26–27
personal responsibility, 36
personnel departments, 78–79
Perverted-Justice.com, 28–29
Phillips, William, 129
physical abuse, 107–108, 108–113
Pistone, Joseph, 40
Pittsburgh Police Department, 132, 141
planted evidence, 120–125
police abuse of authority. *See* abuse of authority
police academies, 32
police brutality, 5, 108–113, 132. *See also* abuse of authority
police-citizen encounters, 107–108, 111
Police Codes of Ethics. *See* Law Enforcement Code of Ethics
police conduct, 4. *See also* police misconduct
police corruption. *See* corruption
police corruption scandals, 75–78, 81–82, 86–87
police department corruption. *See* corrupt police departments
police force, ideal, 10

police groupies, 57
Police Image and Ethics Committee, 17
police interactions, 127
police lying
   accepted lying, 40–43
   to avoid criminal/civil liability, 43–44
   and the Code of Ethics, 39–40
   for a conviction, 113–115
   to cover-up actions, 110
   deviant lying, 43–45
   in support of a perceived legitimate goal, 118–120
   tolerated lying, 43
police misconduct, 5. *See also* police conduct
police officers. *See* law enforcement officers
police pursuits, 111
police reformers, 143
police services, 20
police stings, 63–64
police testimony, 119
police whistleblowers. *See* whistleblowers
policy, 88
Poole, Timothy J., 26
pornography, 56, 57
power of arrest, 20–21
predators, 28–29, 57–58
prescription drugs, 39
pressure from peer group, 101
proactive approach, 103–105, 131
proactive internal policing, 102–103
proactive management oversight, 130–131
proactive policy, 103
procedures for control
   bars, grills, cabarets and bottle clubs, 93
   construction sites, 93–94
   explanation of, 88–89
   gambling, 99
   gypsy or unlicensed cabs, 97
   hotels and restaurants, 94–95
   narcotics, 100–101
   parking lots, 95
   prostitution, 98–99
   repair shops, garages, trucking companies, 96
   tow trucks, 98
   traffic violations, 97
professional development, 36
professional ethics, 15
professional model of policing, 107–108

Professional Performance Enhancement Program (PPEP), 132
prostitution, 56, 57, 98–99
prostitution rings, 65–66
protect and serve, 21
protection of illegal activities, 65–67, 75
protection orders violation, 27–28
protests, 3
provocation, 109, 110, 111
psychological abuse, 107–108
pub bombings, 120
public education, 90
Pulido, Roberto, 69
punishment-oriented approach, 133
pursuits, 111

Q

Queen, Billy, 40
quotas, 124–125, 130

R

racial disparity, 111–112
racial profiling, 142
Rampart corruption incident, 77, 145
Rampart CRASH (specialized gang) unit, 7
Rampart Investigation, 78–79
random interviews, 105–106
Rangel, Charles B., 132
rationalizations, 69–70, 101, 111, 113–114, 117
reactive approach, 131
reactive control, 102–103
reactive internal policing, 102–103
reactive policy, 103
reform administrator, 87
reformers, 143
reform model of policing, 107–108
regulations, 89
relaxed hiring standards, 78–80
Reno, Janet, 132
repair shops, 95–96
resignations, 135–136
resisting arrests, 109, 111
restaurants, 94–95
restrictive concepts, 114
retaliation, 129
review boards, 142

Richardson, James, 116–117
rights violations, 113
riots, 3, 141
River Cops, 76–77, 78
robbery, 70–71
Roebuck, Julian, 60
rogues, 86
Rothstein, Scott, 50–51
rotten apple theory, 74–78, 144
rotten structures, 144
rules, 89
Rules of Conduct (ROC), 89
rule violations. *See* organizational/rule violations

S

safety, 133
Sapp, Allan, 52
Sapp's categories of police sexual misconduct, 52–57
screening process, 126–127
Sease, Arthur, IV, 69
Seattle, Washington, 8
Seattle Police Department, 78
selective enforcement of laws, 32
self-control, 126–127
separation of licensee, 137–138
Serpico, Frank, 130
serve and protect, 21
sexual deviants, 57–58
sexual extortion, 56
sexual harassment. *See* sexual misconduct
sexual misconduct
    assaults, 28
    citizen-initiated sexual contacts, 57
    contacts with crime victims, 53
    contacts with juveniles, 55–56
    contacts with offenders, 53–55
    harassment, 52–53
    indecent exposure, 53
shakedowns, 56–57, 63–65, 75
shame, 129
Shenandoah, Pennsylvania Police Department, 81
shootings, 3, 5, 7, 44–45, 109
Simmons, George, 82, 83, 84
Simpson trial, 118–119
situational lies, 43

social control, 35–36
social interaction, 127
social isolation, 101
socialization process, 127
Spring Lake, North Carolina Police Department, 84
stance of the administrator, 87
standards of conduct. *See* ethical standards
Statement of Ethical Principles, 17–18
status, 25
Stephens, D. W., 38
steroids, 39
Steubenville, Ohio, 141
sting operations, 106
straight shooters, 85–86
stream video system, 132–133
stress, 103
strippers, 56
subjective test, 41
Sullivan City, Texas Police Department, 91
supervision increases, 91
supervisory control, 130
supervisory failures, 141
Supreme Court decisions, 23
surveillance videotapes, 5, 8, 133

T

Tarnished Blue Task Force, 113
TASER, 4–5
task forces, 72
tax collections, 65
taxis, 96–97
technical assists, 132–133
Tennessee v. Garner, 112
terminations, 135–136
testifying, 128
testilying, 119
testimony by police, 119
Texas Commission on Law Enforcement Officer Standards and Education, 137–138, 138–140
thefts, opportunistic, 61–63
third-degree interrogation techniques, 113–114
threat to homeland security, 72
Timoney, John, 50
tolerated lying, 43
tow trucks, 97–98

traffic control, 21
traffic ticket fixes, 66–67
traffic violations, 97
traffic violators, 64
training, 12–13, 14, 145–146
traitor, 128
trucking companies, 95–96
trust, 35–36
Tulia, Texas, 136–137
turnarounds, 105
Typology of Disinterested Rules Violations, 114

U

undercover officers, 40–42, 104, 105
undercover techniques, 136
unethical behavior, 3, 6, 9
United Kingdom conviction, 120
United Nations Police Task Force, 18
unlicensed cabs, 96–97
untrustworthy, 30
U.S. Attorney General, 111
USA v Scott Rothstein, 50–51
U.S. Department of Justice, 4, 7, 132, 142
use of force, 11–12. *See also* excessive force
U.S. Government Accounting Office, 132
U.S. Supreme Court, 112
Utah Post, 52

V

values, 127
verbal abuse, 109
verbals, 115–116
vice operations, 65, 74
victimless crimes, 65
video feeds, 132–133
violation of protection orders, 27–28
violence, domestic. *See* domestic violence
Violent Crime Control and Law Enforcement Act, 111
Vollmer, August, 116
voyeuristic contacts, 53

W

Walker, S., 22
Ward, Richard H., 91
war on drugs. *See* drug-related crimes

War Theory of Crime Control, 113–115
Washington, D.C., 79, 129
Washington, Seattle, 8
weapon for administration, 133–134
Webb, Lt., 83
Welfel, E. F., 130
West New York, 81–82
Whistleblower Reinforcement Act, 129
whistleblowers, 128, 129
white knights, 85
"white lies," 43
Whitman, Charles, 26

Wickersham Commission, 113–114
wire fraud, 29
Witham, Donald, 13
Wren, T. E., 129

Y

YouTube, 3

Z

zero-tolerance policing, 112

Charles C Thomas
PUBLISHER • LTD.

P.O. Box 19265
Springfield, IL 62794-9265

- Mendell, Ronald L.—**THE QUIET THREAT: Fighting Industrial Espionage in America. (2nd Ed.)** '11, 254 pp. (7 x 10), 4 il., 6 tables.

- Bartone, Paul T., & Bjorn Helge Johnsen, Jarle Eid, John M. Violanti & Jon Christian Laberg—**ENHANCING HUMAN PERFORMANCE IN SECURITY OPERATIONS: International and Law Enforcement Perspectives.** '10, 264 pp. (7 x 10), 23 il, 15 tables.

- Carelli, Anne O'Brien—**THE TRUTH ABOUT SUPERVISION: Coaching, Teamwork, Interviewing, Appraisals, 360° Assessments, Delegation, and Recognition. (2nd Ed.)** '10, 232 pp. (7 x 10), 33 il., (and a CD ROM containing 33 Self-Assessment Tools), paper.

- Covey, Herbert C.—**STREET GANGS THROUGHOUT THE WORLD. (2nd Ed.)** '10, 328 pp. (7 x 10), 1 table, $63.95, hard, $43.95, paper.

- Garner, Gerald W.—**POLICE CHIEF 101: Practical Advice for the Law Enforcement Leader.** '10, 284 pp. (7 x 10), $60.95, hard, $40.95, paper.

- Hale, Charles D.—**THE ASSESSMENT CENTER HANDBOOK FOR POLICE AND FIRE PERSONNEL. (3rd Ed.)** '10, 240 pp. (7 x 10), 64 il., spiral, paper.

- Hendricks, James E., Jerome B. McKean, & Cindy Gillespie Hendricks—**CRISIS INTERVENTION: Contemporary Issues for On-Site Interveners. (4th Ed.)** '10, 384 pp. (7 x 10), 4 il., 1 table.

- McDevitt, Daniel S. & Mark W. Field—**POLICE CHIEF: How to Attain and Succeed in this Critical Position.** '10, 306 pp. (7 x 10), 2 il.

- Mendell, Ronald L.—**PROBING INTO COLD CASES: A Guide for Investigators.** '10, 324 pp. (7 x 10), 5 il., 34 tables, $63.95, hard, $43.95, paper.

- Slatkin, Arthur A.—**COMMUNICATION IN CRISIS AND HOSTAGE NEGOTIATIONS: Practical Communication Techniques, Stratagems, and Strategies for Law Enforcement, Corrections, and Emergency Service Personnel in Managing Critical Incidents. (2nd Ed.)** '10, 230 pp. (7 x 10), $39.95, spiral (paper).

- Weiss, Peter A.—**PERSONALITY ASSESSMENT IN POLICE PSYCHOLOGY: A 21ST Century Perspective.** '10, 402 pp., (7 x 10), 70 il., 26 tables, $79.95, hard, $55.95, paper.

- Yereance, Robert A, & Todd Kerkhoff—**ELECTRICAL FIRE ANALYSIS. (3rd Ed.)** '10, 338 pp. (7 x 10), 14 il., 4 tables.

- Axelrod, Evan M.—**VIOLENCE GOES TO THE INTERNET: Avoiding the Snare of the Net.** '09, 406 pp. (7 x 10), 17 il., 39 tables, $82.95, hard, $56.95, paper.

- Colaprete, Frank A.—**MENTORING IN THE CRIMINAL JUSTICE PROFESSIONS: Conveyance of the Craft.** '09, 310 pp. (7 x 10), $62.95, hard, $42.95, paper.

- Gilly, Thomas Albert, Yakov Gilinskiy & Vladimir A. Sergevnin—**THE ETHICS OF TERRORISM: Innovative Approaches from an International Perspective (17 Lectures).** '09, 250 pp. (7 x 10), 8 il., 9 tables, $62.95, hard, $42.95, paper.

- McDevitt, Daniel S.—**MAJOR CASE MANAGEMENT: A Guide for Law Enforcement Managers.** '09, 270 pp. (7 x 10), $59.95, hard, $39.95, paper.

- Wadman, Robert C.—**POLICE THEORY IN AMERICA: Old Traditions and New Opportunities.** '09, 198 pp. (7 x 10) 18 il., $49.95, hard, $29.95, paper.

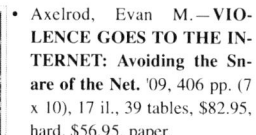

- MacKinem, Mitchell, B. & Paul Higgins—**DRUG COURT: Constructing the Moral Identity of Drug Offenders.** '08, 190 pp. (7 x 10), 1 il., 2 tables, $49.95, hard, $33.95, paper.

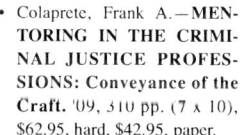

- Mijares, Tomas C. & Ronald M. McCarthy—**THE MANAGEMENT OF POLICE SPECIALIZED TACTICAL UNITS. (2nd Ed.)** '08, 308 pp. (7 x 10), 2 tables, $64.95, hard, $44.95, paper.

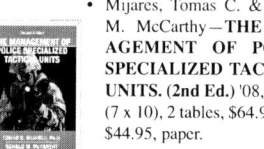

- More, Harry W.—**CURRENT ISSUES IN AMERICAN LAW ENFORCEMENT: Controversies and Solutions.** '08, 302 pp. (7 x 10), 24 il., 20 tables, $63.95, hard, $43.95, paper.

- Thomas, Robert G. & R. Murray Thomas—**EFFECTIVE TEACHING IN CORRECTIONAL SETTINGS. Prisons, Jails, Juvenile Centers, and Alternative Schools.** '08, 246 pp. (7 x 10), 10 il., 4 tables, $55.95, hard, $35.95, paper.

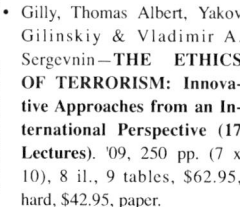

- Urbina, Martin Guevara—**A COMPREHENSIVE STUDY OF FEMALE OFFENDERS: Life Before, During, and After Incarceration.** '08, 294 pp. (7 x 10), 27 tables, $62.95, hard, $42.95, paper.

- Payne, Brian K.—**CRIME AND ELDER ABUSE: An Integrated Perspective. (2nd Ed.)** '05, 332 pp. (7 x 10), 7 il., 18 tables, $69.95, hard, $49.95, paper.

5 easy ways to order!

PHONE: 1-800-258-8980 or (217) 789-8980
FAX: (217) 789-9130
EMAIL: books@ccthomas.com
Web: www.ccthomas.com
MAIL: Charles C Thomas • Publisher, Ltd. P.O. Box 19265 Springfield, IL 62794-9265

Complete catalog available at www.ccthomas.com or email books@ccthomas.com

Books sent on approval • Shipping charges: $7.75 min. U.S. / Outside U.S., actual shipping fees will be charged • Prices subject to change without notice